one more skein

30 Quick Projects to Knit

LEIGH RADFORD

photography by John Mulligan

STC CRAFT | A MELANIE FALICK BOOK

Stewart, Tabori & Chang • New York

Published in 2009 by Stewart, Tabori & Chang
An imprint of Harry N. Abrams, Inc.

Text copyright © 2009 by Leigh Radford
Photographs copyright © 2009 by John Mulligan

Library of Congress Cataloging-in-Publication Data:
Radford, Leigh.
One more skein : 30 quick projects to knit / Leigh Radford ; photography
by John Mulligan.
     p. cm.
ISBN 978-1-58479-802-6
1. Knitting—Patterns. I. Title.
TT825.R284 2009
746.43'2046—dc22
2008049040

Editor: Melanie Falick
Designer: Anna Christian
Production Manager: Jacqueline Poirier

The text of this book was composed in Neutraface.

Printed and bound in China

10 9 8 7 6 5 4 3 2 1

HNA
harry n. abrams, inc.
a subsidiary of La Martinière Groupe

115 West 18th Street
New York, NY 10011
www.hnabooks.com

Contents

Introduction

While I have always kept paint, drawing pencils, and a sketchbook close at hand, for most of the last decade I've been more focused on knitwear design than painting and drawing. For a long period I didn't really see a connection between these two sides of my creativity. But around the time that I started working on this book, I also enrolled in art school. Early on in my classes I began exploring how I might incorporate knitting into my paintings, for example, by knitting my own canvas out of laceweight linen. And now when I review the collection of projects that I've put together for this book, I clearly see that what I am learning in art class is seeping into and re-energizing my knitting.

In both areas, I am exploring ways to create aesthetically beautiful works as simply and cleanly as possible. These days when I come up with an idea, I ask myself if there is a way to pare it down in order to enrich it. The Pleated Vase Sleeve (page 107), for example, is a simple vessel "embellished" with only a few strategically placed pleats. The Mikus Linen Placemats (page 113) are my study of light and shadow. The Rosette Stitch Cowl (page 25) makes lace look simple and bold rather than intricate and delicate, thanks to large needles and bulky yarn.

In my book *One Skein*, I included only projects that could be completed with one skein of yarn. For *One More Skein*, I gave myself slightly more leeway: All of the projects are made with one or two skeins of yarn except for the Albers Stash Blanket (page 100), which is made with leftovers of many different colors (and is named for the acclaimed abstract painter and color theorist Josef Albers). I set out to develop classic projects that would be fun but not difficult to knit (and, depending on one's level of experience, might introduce a new technique), beautiful to look at, and useful for oneself or as a gift. Very few of them are worked at a small gauge, so they are quick to knit. There are quite a few projects for baby since, obviously, baby clothes require a minimal amount of yarn (often they can be made with leftovers from other larger projects), and because most knitters do tend to enjoy dressing up babies in handknits.

My favorite part of designing the projects for this book was the beginning, when I was sketching, swatching, and problem solving. Often I started with a simple concept instead of a particular type of project in mind. For example, I spent time sketching squares, manipulating them on a page, not at all sure where I was headed, before deciding that they would become the central motif of the Connected Squares Felted Handbag (page 79). For Sadie's Capelet (page 46), I spent time exploring the visual and textural relationships between ribbing and cables. In many cases, once I decided what I was going to make and figured out how to achieve my goals, I felt like I was finished. But, of course, I needed to knit the real piece and, a few times, I did alter my plans during that time. For example, as I was knitting the Circle and Stripe Cravat (page 28) I decided to devote more space to the cable circles than to the rib pattern so that when worn, the design would be asymmetrical.

The key to all of this was taking time to explore the creative process. That was a gift to myself, the same gift that I hope you will give to yourself, perhaps inspired not only by the projects you see here but by my experience of delving into other areas of artistic expression outside of knitting in order to refresh my perspective on knitting.

Two needles and one (or one more) skein of yarn—the possibilities never cease to amaze me.

1 PUT IT ON

Fingerless Gloves

I love fingerless gloves and believe that you can't have too many pairs. I designed these after an early-morning bike ride during which my arms were a little chilly but the rest of my body was just fine (thus a jacket would have been overkill). They are worked flat, then sewn up the side, with a space left open for the thumb. You choose whether you want long gloves (see left) or short or striped ones (see pages 14 and 15). You can also choose which side of the rib pattern you want to be the public side or, if you are careful with your side seams, you can make them reversible.

SIZES
Small (Medium, Large)

Shown in size Large

FINISHED MEASUREMENTS
5 ¼ (5 ¾, 6 ½)" hand circumference

8 ½" long, Short Gloves

12 ½" long, Long Gloves

YARN
See page 14.

NEEDLES
One pair straight needles size US 8 (5 mm)

One pair straight needles size US 10 (6 mm)

Change needle size if necessary to obtain correct gauge.

GAUGE
20 sts and 22 rows = 4" (10 cm) in 3×1 Rib, using larger needles

24 sts and 26 rows = 4" (10 cm) in 3×1 Rib, using smaller needles

STITCH PATTERNS

3×1 Rib
(multiple of 4 sts + 3; 1-row repeat)

Row 1 (WS): P3, *k1, p3; repeat from * to end.

Row 2: Knit the knit sts and purl the purl sts as they face you.

Repeat Row 2 for 3×1 Rib.

Stripe Pattern
*Note: For Short Gloves, begin Stripe Pattern at *.*

For Left Hand, work 3 rows A; [2 rows B; 2 rows A] 3 times; 6 rows B; 2 rows A; *2 rows B; 2 rows A; 2 rows B; 4 rows A; 2 rows B; 2 rows A; 4 rows B; 6 rows A; [2 rows B; 2 rows A] twice; 2 rows B; 4 rows A; 4 rows B; 2 rows A. BO with last color used. For Right Hand, reverse colors, working A instead of B and vice versa.

GLOVES

Short Gloves
Using smaller needles and A, CO 31 (35, 39) sts, leaving 15" tail.

YARN

LONG GLOVES: **Artyarns Ultramerino 8 (100% merino wool; 188 yards / 100 grams): 2 hanks #UM122.** *Note: If working with yarn from your stash, you will need approximately 310 (345, 376) yards.*

LONG STRIPED GLOVES: **Cascade 220 Heathers (100% Peruvian highland merino wool; 220 yards / 100 grams): 1 hank each #4005 (A) and #9327 (B).** *Note: If working with yarn from your stash, you will need approximately 68 (76, 85) yards A and 62 (70, 77) yards B.*

SHORT GLOVES: **Cascade 220 Heathers (100% Peruvian highland merino wool; 220 yards / 100 grams): 1 hank #9327.** *Note: If working with yarn from your stash, you will need approximately 78 (84, 95) yards. This pair was sewn together with the WS of the rib pattern facing out.*

SHORT STRIPED GLOVES (not shown): **Cascade 220 Heathers (100% Peruvian highland merino wool; 220 yards / 100 grams): 1 hank each A and B.** *Note: If working with yarn from your stash, you will need approximately 41 (44, 49) yards A and 37 (40, 45) yards B.*

Begin 3×1 Rib; work even until piece measures 8½" from the beginning, ending with a WS row. BO all sts in rib.

Long Gloves

Using larger needles and A, CO 31 (35, 39) sts, leaving 15" tail. Begin 3×1 Rib; work even until piece measures 7½" from the beginning, ending with a WS row. Change to smaller needles; work even until piece measures 12½" from the beginning, ending with a WS row. BO all sts in rib.

Striped Gloves

Work as for Short or Long Gloves, casting on using A for Left Glove and B for Right Glove, and following Stripe Pattern, beginning where indicated for Short Gloves.

FINISHING

Using BO tail, sew side seam from BO edge to just above where you want thumb opening to begin. Sew side seam from CO edge to just below thumb, trying on Glove and adjusting thumb opening as desired. *Note: The Short Gloves shown were sewn together with the WS of the rib pattern facing out.*

Weave in loose ends. Block to measurements.

Top-Down Earflap Hat

This hat is so quick to knit you'll have one ready for each member of the family in no time. Functional and fashionable, it's a must-have for cold weather.

SIZES
3X-Small (2X-Small, X-Small, Small, Medium, Large)

To fit infant (toddler, child, adult small, adult medium, adult large)

Shown in size Large.

FINISHED
MEASUREMENTS
14¼ (16, 17¾, 19½, 21¼, 23)" circumference

YARN
Malabrigo Yarn Chunky (100% merino wool; 104 yards / 3½ ounces): 1 hank #130 Damask

NEEDLES
One set of five double-pointed needles (dpn) size US 10½ (6.5 mm)

Change needle size if necessary to obtain correct gauge.

NOTIONS
Stitch marker; stitch holder or waste yarn

GAUGE
13½ sts and 23½ rows = 4" (10 cm) in Stockinette stitch (St st)

HAT

CO 8 sts. Divide sts evenly among 4 dpn. Join for working in the rnd, being careful not to twist sts; place marker (pm) for beginning of rnd. Knit 1 rnd.

Shape Hat

Rnd 1: *K1, M1; repeat from * to end—16 sts.

Rnd 2: *K2, M1; repeat from * to end—24 sts.

Rnd 3: K2, *M1, k4; repeat from * to last 2 sts, M1, k2—30 sts.

Rnd 4: *K5, M1; repeat from * to end—36 sts.

Rnd 5: *K6, M1; repeat from * to end—42 sts.

Rnd 6: Knit.

Rnd 7: *K7, M1; repeat from * to end—48 sts.

Rnd 8: Knit.

Sizes 2X-Small, X-Small, Small, Medium, and Large Only
Rnd 9: *K8, M1; repeat from * to end—54 sts.

Rnd 10: Knit.

Sizes X-Small, Small, Medium, and Large Only
Rnd 11: *K9, M1; repeat from * to end—60 sts.

Rnd 12: Knit.

Sizes Small, Medium, and Large Only

Rnd 13: *K10, M1; repeat from * to end—66 sts.

Rnd 14: Knit.

Sizes Medium and Large Only

Rnd 15: *K11, M1; repeat from * to end—72 sts.

Rnd 16: Knit.

Size Large Only

Rnd 17: *K12, M1; repeat from * to end—78 sts.

Rnd 18: Knit.

All Sizes

Work even for 3 (3¼, 3¼, 3½, 3½, 3¾)", or until piece reaches top of ears.

Shape Earflaps

Next Rnd: BO 14 (17, 18, 19, 20, 23) sts purlwise, k10 (10, 12, 14, 16, 16) for Earflap, BO next 14 (17, 18, 19, 20, 23) sts purlwise, k10 (10, 12, 14, 16, 16) for second Earflap. Transfer first Earflap sts to st holder or waste yarn. Working back and forth on sts for second Earflap, work as follows:

Row 1 and all WS rows: K1, purl to last st, k1.

Row 2: Knit.

Row 4 (Decrease Row): K1, ssk, knit to last 3 sts, k2tog, k1—8 (8, 10, 12, 14, 14) sts remain.

Repeat Decrease Row every 4 rows 2 (2, 2, 1, 0, 0) time(s), then every other row 0 (0, 1, 3, 5, 5) times, ending with a WS row—4 sts remain.

Next Row (RS): K1, k2tog, k1—3 sts remain.

Work I-Cord (see Special Techniques, page 120) on remaining sts until I-Cord measures approximately 5". BO all sts.

Repeat for second Earflap.

FINISHING

Weave in loose ends. Block lightly.

Linen Cap

Worked in linen yarn rather than the more typical wool, this cap works especially well in warm climates. Ribbon worked through eyelets at the bottom edge can be used to adjust fit or just as a decoration.

SIZES
Small (Medium, Large, X-Large)

Shown in sizes Medium and Large

FINISHED MEASUREMENTS
18 (19 ¾, 21½, 23¼)" circumference

YARN
Louet Euroflax Light Worsted Weight (100% linen; 190 yards / 100 grams): 1 hank #43 Pewter (shown in size Medium) or #48 Aqua (shown in size Large)

NEEDLES
One 16" (40 cm) long circular (circ) needle size US 3 (3.25 mm)

Change needle size if necessary to obtain correct gauge.

NOTIONS
Stitch markers; ½ yard ½" wide ribbon

GAUGE
28 sts and 40 rows = 4" (10 cm) in Stockinette stitch (St st)

BRIM

CO 84 (92, 100, 108) sts. Join for working in the rnd, being careful not to twist sts; place marker (pm) for beginning of rnd. Purl 4 rnds. Knit 3 rnds.

Eyelet Rnd: *K2, k2tog, yo; repeat from * to end. Change to St st (knit every rnd); work even for 3 rnds.

Increase Rnd: *K2, M1; repeat from * to end—126 (138, 150, 162) sts. Work even until piece measures approximately 5 (5½, 6, 6½)" from the beginning (with edge unrolled), decreasing 1 (3, 0, 2) sts on last rnd—125 (135, 150, 160) sts remain.

CROWN

Decrease Rnd 1: *K2tog, k21 (23, 26, 28), ssk, pm; repeat from * to end—115 (125, 140, 150) sts remain. Knit 1 rnd.

Decrease Rnd 2: *K2tog, knit to 2 sts before next marker, ssk, slip marker (sm); repeat from * to end—105 (115, 130, 140) sts remain. Knit 1 rnd.

Repeat Decrease Rnd 2 every other rnd 9 (10, 11, 12) times—15 (15, 20, 20) sts remain.

Sizes Small and Medium Only
Decrease Rnd 3: *K2tog, k1; repeat from * to end—10 sts remain.

Sizes Large and X-Large Only
Decrease Rnd 3: *K2tog, ssk; repeat from * to end—10 sts remain.

All Sizes
Decrease Rnd 4: *K2tog; repeat from * to end—5 sts remain.

Break yarn, leaving a long tail. Thread tail through remaining sts, pull tight, and fasten off.

FINISHING
Weave in loose ends. Block to measurements.

Thread ribbon through Eyelet Rnd. Tie in a bow.

Felted Cuff

I always enjoy the process of manipulating fabric to affect its look, feel, and finished size. Here I knitted a basic cuff, felted it, and then while it was still wet, created the pleats at the top. Once dry, I added a length of leather lacing to keep the pleats snug.

FINISHED MEASUREMENTS

16" circumference at widest point × 3¾" high, before felting

Approximately 10½" circumference × 2½" high, after felting and pleating

Note: Results will depend on felting conditions and time spent felting.

YARN

ShibuiKnits Merino Alpaca (50% baby alpaca / 50% merino wool; 131 yards / 100 grams): 1 hank #MA1395 Honey

NEEDLES

One set of five double-pointed needles (dpn) size US 10½ (6.5 mm)

Change needle size if necessary to obtain correct gauge.

NOTIONS

U or T pins; sharp tapestry needle; masking tape; 15" leather cord

GAUGE

16 sts and 19 rnds = 4" (10 cm) in Stockinette stitch (St st), before felting

CUFF

CO 48 sts. Join for working in the rnd, being careful not to twist sts; place marker (pm) for beginning of rnd. Knit 5 rnds.

Increase Rnd: *K2, k1-f/b; repeat from * to end—64 sts. Knit 5 rnds.

Decrease Rnd: *K2, k2tog, k2, ssk; repeat from * to end—48 sts remain. Knit 4 rnds. BO all sts.

FINISHING

Weave in loose ends.

Felting: Felt Cuff to desired dimensions (see Special Techniques, page 120). Using U or T pins, create pleats. Allow to air-dry completely before removing pins.

ASSEMBLY

Once Cuff is completely dry, thread leather cord onto tapestry needle. Place piece of masking tape at one end of leather cord to prevent cord from pulling all the way through the pleats. Insert needle through pleats from right to left, 1" below top of Cuff, leaving 2" tail, then back in opposite direction, ⅛" below first pass, leaving 3" loop on left-hand side of Cuff. Loop should be long enough to reach across pleats and catch knot on opposite side. Remove needle and tape from cord. With both ends of cord held together, tie knot in end, adjusting length of loop as necessary, so that Cuff fits comfortably. Trim ends ¼" from knot.

Rosette Stitch Cowl

I like the way a cowl keeps you warm without the extra fabric of a scarf or wrap. To create this one, I played with proportion and scale, matching a bulky yarn and very large needles with a lacy openwork pattern.

FINISHED MEASUREMENTS
23" circumference × 11" long

YARN
Blue Sky Alpacas Bulky (50% alpaca / 50% wool; 45 yards / 100 grams): 2 hanks #1213 Jasmine

NEEDLES
One pair straight needles size US 35 (19 mm)

Change needle size if necessary to obtain correct gauge.

GAUGE
6¼ sts and 8 rows = 4" (10 cm) in Rosette Stitch

STITCH PATTERN

Rosette Stitch
(even number of sts; 4-row repeat)

Rows 1 and 3 (RS): Knit.

Row 2: P1, *p2tog, leaving sts on needle; knit these same sts tbl, slipping sts from needle together; repeat from * to last st, p1.

Row 4: P2, *p2tog, leaving sts on needle; knit these same sts tbl, slipping sts from needle together; repeat from * to last 2 sts, p2.

Repeat Rows 1–4 for Rosette Stitch.

COWL
CO 36 sts. Begin Rosette st; work even until piece measures 11" from the beginning, ending with a WS row. BO all sts in pattern. Break yarn, leaving a 15" tail.

FINISHING
Using Mattress st (see Special Techniques, page 120), sew side seam, leaving last 5" unsewn. Weave in loose ends. Block to measurements.

Horizontal Rib Scarf

It's all in how you look at it ... or in which direction you look. This scarf is actually worked side-to-side rather than in a long vertical strip as is more typical. While I chose to make this one in a solid color, a striped version will definitely be on my knitting needles soon.

FINISHED MEASUREMENTS
102" wide × 4 1/2" long

YARN
Malabrigo Yarn Worsted (100% merino wool; 215 yards / 100 grams): 2 hanks #52 Paris Night

NEEDLES
One 32" (80 cm) long or longer circular (circ) needle size US 10 (6 mm)

Change needle size if necessary to obtain correct gauge.

GAUGE
18 sts and 23 rows = 4" (10 cm) in scarf pattern

SCARF
CO 460 sts.

Rows 1, 3, 5, 7, and 9 (WS): P3, *k6, p2; repeat from * to last 9 sts, k6, p3.

Rows 2, 4, 6, and 8: K3, *p6, k2; repeat from * to last 9 sts, p6, k3.

Rows 10, 12, 14, and 16: K3, *p2, k2; repeat from * to last 5 sts, p2, k3.

Rows 11, 13, 15, and 17: P3, *k2, p2; repeat from * to last 5 sts, k2, p3.

Rows 18, 20, 22, and 24: K3, p2, *k2, p6; repeat from * to last 7 sts, k2, p2, k3.

Rows 19, 21, 23, and 25: P3, k2, *p2, k6; repeat from * to last 7 sts, p2, k2, p3.

BO all sts in pattern.

FINISHING
Weave in loose ends. Block to measurements.

Circle & Stripe Scarf & Cravat

The work of two sculptors, Norman Carlberg and Erwin Hauer, inspired me to explore the use of line and form in my knitting. Here's one of the results: a scarf (see right) and cravat (see page 30) that pair vertical lines and circles. I am especially pleased with the way the circle pattern close to the edge creates a gentle scallop that effectively juxtaposes the strong vertical lines of the opposite border.

FINISHED MEASUREMENTS
SCARF: 6 ¾" wide × 64" long

CRAVAT: 5 ½" wide × 30 ½" long

YARN
SCARF: Malabrigo Yarn Worsted (100% merino; 215 yards / 100 grams): 2 hanks #23 Pagoda or #56 Olive

CRAVAT: Malabrigo Yarn Worsted (100% merino; 215 yards / 100 grams): 2 hanks #123 Rhodesian

NEEDLES
One pair straight needles size US 9 (5.5 mm)

Change needle size if necessary to obtain correct gauge.

NOTIONS
Cable needle (cn)

GAUGE
22 sts and 23 rows = 4" (10 cm) in Cable Pattern from Scarf Chart

SCARF
CO 43 sts.

Begin Chart (WS): Work Rows 1–17 of Chart once, then repeat Rows 2–17 until piece measures 64" from the beginning, ending with Row 17. BO all sts in pattern.

FINISHING
Weave in loose ends. Block to measurements.

CRAVAT

STITCH PATTERN

2×2 Rib
(multiple of 4 sts + 2; 1-row repeat)

Row 1 (RS): *K2, p2; repeat from * to last 2 sts, k2.

Row 2: Knit the knit sts and purl the purl sts as they face you.

Repeat Row 2 for 2×2 Rib.

CRAVAT

CO 34 sts. Purl 1 row.

Begin Chart (RS): Work Rows 1-16 of Chart until piece measures approximately 20¾" from the beginning, ending with Row 7.

Next Row (WS): Purl, increase 8 sts evenly across row—42 sts.

Next Row (RS): Change to 2×2 Rib. Work even for 4½", ending with a WS row.

Shape Slits (RS): Work 18 sts, join a second ball of yarn, work 6 sts, join a third ball of yarn, work to end. Working three sections at the same time, work even until slits measure 2", ending with a WS row.

Next Row (RS): Work across all sts, dropping second and third balls. Work even until piece measures 30½" from the beginning. BO all sts in pattern.

FINISHING

Weave in loose ends. Block to measurements.

SCARF CHART

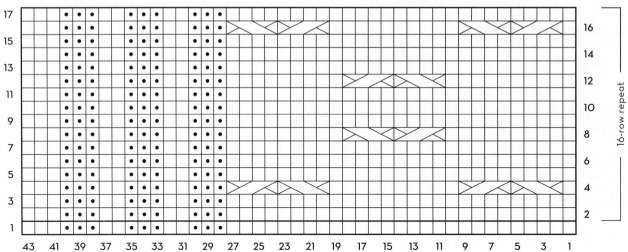

CRAVAT CHART

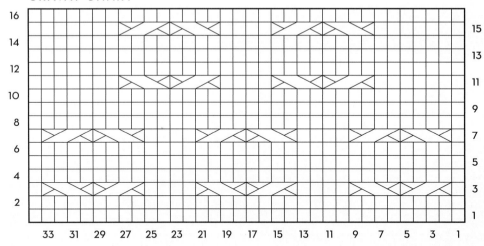

KEY

☐ Knit on RS, purl on WS.

⊡ Purl on RS, knit on WS.

⧄ Slip 2 sts to cn, hold to back, k2, k2 from cn.

⧅ Slip 2 sts to cn, hold to front, k2, k2 from cn.

FINISHED
MEASUREMENTS
EARRINGS: Approximately 2"
long

BRACELET: Approximately 7"
long, not including clasp

NECKLACE: Approximately 14"
long, not including clasp

YARN
Lanaknits Allhemp6 (100%
hemp; 165 yards / 100 grams):
1 hank #23 Brick Note: Earrings,
Bracelet, and Necklace use
approximately 3, 14, and 50
yards, respectively.

NEEDLES
One pair straight needles in
each of these sizes: US 2 (2.75
mm), US 3 (3.25 mm), and US 5
(3.75 mm)

One pair double-pointed
needles (dpn) size US 3
(3.25 mm)

NOTIONS
Waste yarn in sport or DK
weight; stitch holders; forty-two
10 mm nickel or sterling silver
closed jump rings for Earrings,
three 18 mm open jump rings
for Bracelet, forty-three 18 mm
closed jump rings for Necklace;
earring wires with jump ring
attached; lobster clasp with
jump rings attached for Bracelet;
clasp for Necklace; 2 pair
small pliers (see Sources for
Supplies, page 124, for all
jewelry supplies)

GAUGE
Gauge not critical.

Jewelry Trio

I like using hemp for knitted jewelry because it holds its shape well and creates a smooth, interesting surface for embellishments. Here I've elevated utilitarian jump rings, typically employed to connect pieces of jewelry to their clasps, to decorative "bead" status.

EARRINGS

Using dpn, CO 2 sts. Work I-Cord (see Special Techniques, page 120) for 3¾". BO all sts, leaving 4" tail. Slip 21 jump rings onto I-Cord. Sew ends of I-Cord together and, using tail, create small loop for earring wire at seam, making sure loop is well anchored. Open jump ring in earring wire (see Special Techniques, page 120), slip yarn loop onto jump ring; close ring.

BRACELET

Note: Side edges will roll into the center as you work.

Using size US 3 straight needles and waste yarn, CO 3 sts. Change to working yarn, leaving 12" tail. Begin St st; work even for 2 rows.

Shape Bracelet
Increase Row (RS): K1, M1, work to last st, M1, k1—5 sts. Work even for 1 row.

Repeat Increase Row every other row 5 times—15 sts. Work even for 2" or to half of desired length, ending with a WS row. *Note: Deduct length of lobster clasp from desired total length.*

Decrease Row (RS): K1, ssk, work to last 3 sts, k2tog, k1—13 sts remain. Work even for 1 row.

Repeat Decrease Row every other row 4 times—5 sts remain.

Next Row (RS): K1, slip 1, k2tog, psso, k1—3 sts remain. Work even for 3 rows.

Transfer remaining sts to st holder. Break yarn, leaving 12" tail.

FINISHING

Open jump ring of lobster clasp (see Special Techniques, page 120); slip first and last sts from holder onto jump ring; close ring. Open second jump ring of lobster clasp. Carefully unpick waste yarn and slip sts onto jump ring; close ring.Open the three 18 mm jump rings as for clasp and secure around center of Bracelet (see photo). Wrap tail several times around each end of Bracelet, just below sts on jump ring; secure ends inside wraps.

NECKLACE

Slip 43 jump rings onto working yarn. Using size US 3 straight needles and waste yarn, CO 43 sts. Change to smallest needles and Rev St st; work even for 3 rows, beginning with a purl row. Change to size US 3 needles; work even for 2 rows. Change to largest needles; work even for 2 rows.

Place Jump Rings (WS): *Slip 1 jump ring into position up next to left-hand needle, k1 but do not slip st from needle; slip st just worked back to left-hand needle, k2tog-tbl (st just worked together with next st on needle); repeat from * to end. All jump rings should now be on right-hand needle.

Next Row (RS): Change to size US 3 needles. BO all sts knitwise. Weave in loose ends.

Carefully unpick waste yarn and place sts on size US 3 needle; set aside. Using dpn, CO 2 sts, leaving 4" tail. Work I-Cord (see Special Techniques, page 120) for 3½". Change to Applied I-Cord (see Special Techniques, page 120); work across sts from CO edge of Necklace. Change to free I-Cord; work even for 3½". BO all sts. Break yarn, leaving 4" tail. Thread tail through jump ring or opening of clasp, then back into I-Cord, securing well. Repeat for opposite side.

2 DRESS UP BABY

Baby's Britches

Made with machine-washable organic cotton, these britches are a soft and comfy addition to baby's wardrobe.

SIZES
0–3 months (3–6 months, 6–12 months)

Shown in size 3–6 months

FINISHED MEASUREMENTS
14 1/2 (16 3/4, 18 1/2)" waist

YARN
Blue Sky Alpacas Dyed Cotton (100% organically grown cotton; 150 yards / 100 grams): 2 hanks #634 Periwinkle

NEEDLES
One pair straight needles size US 8 (5 mm)

One 16" (40 cm) long circular (circ) needle size US 8 (5 mm)

One 16" (40 cm) long circular needle size US 7 (4.5 mm)

Change needle size if necessary to obtain correct gauge.

NOTIONS
Stitch markers; stitch holders; 17" long 1" wide non-roll elastic; sewing needle and thread

GAUGE
20 sts and 26 rows = 4" (10 cm) in Stockinette stitch (St st), using larger needles

LEG

Using straight needles, CO 40 (44, 48) sts. Begin St st, beginning with a purl row; work even for 3 rows.

Next Row (RS): K1, *p2, k2; repeat from * to last 3 sts, p2, k1.

Next Row: Knit the knit sts and purl the purl sts as they face you.

Change to St st; work even until piece measures 4 1/2" from the beginning, ending with a WS row.

Shape Leg (RS): Increase 1 st each side this row, then every 6 rows 2 (3, 3) times—46 (52, 56) sts. Work even until piece measures 7 1/2 (8 1/4, 9)" from the beginning, ending with a WS row. Transfer sts to st holder; set aside. Repeat for second Leg; leave sts on needle.

BODY

With RS facing, using larger circ needle, knit across 23 (26, 28) sts of first Leg from holder, place marker (pm) for side of Leg, knit to end of first Leg, knit across 23 (26, 28) sts of second Leg, pm for side of Leg, knit to end—92 (104, 112) sts. Join for working in the rnd; pm for beginning of rnd. Continuing in St st (knit every rnd), work even for 9 (11, 13) rnds.

Shape Body: Decrease 4 sts this rnd, then every 6 rnds 4 times, as follows: [Knit to 3 sts before marker, k2tog, k1, slip marker (sm), k1, ssk] twice, knit to end—72 (84, 92) sts remain. Work even until piece measures 6 1/4 (7, 8)" from join. Purl 1 rnd (turning rnd).

Next Rnd: Change to smaller circ needle. Work even in St st for 1". BO all sts.

FINISHING

Block piece to measurements. Sew inseams. Fold facing over to WS at turning rnd and sew in place, leaving 1" opening, and being careful not to let sts show on RS. Thread elastic through waistband. Overlap ends of elastic and sew together with sewing needle and thread. Sew opening in facing closed. Weave in loose ends.

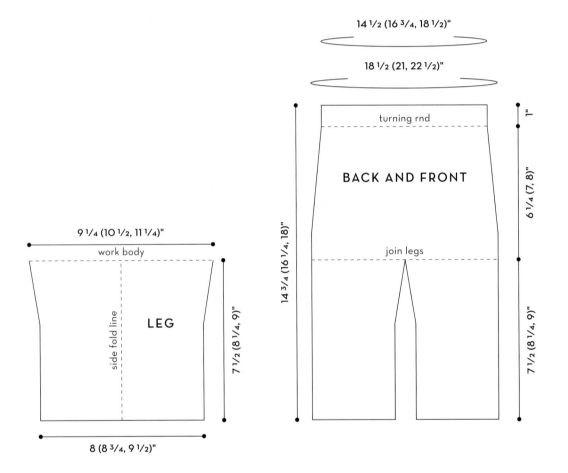

14 1/2 (16 3/4, 18 1/2)"

18 1/2 (21, 22 1/2)"

turning rnd

BACK AND FRONT

1"

6 1/4 (7, 8)"

join legs

14 3/4 (16 1/4, 18)"

7 1/2 (8 1/4, 9)"

9 1/4 (10 1/2, 11 1/4)"

work body

side fold line

LEG

7 1/2 (8 1/4, 9)"

8 (8 3/4, 9 1/2)"

Nash's Garter-Stitch Baby Sweater

Garter stitch and simple construction: the perfect recipe for a quick, cozy baby sweater.

SIZES
0–6 months

FINISHED
MEASUREMENTS
21½" chest

YARN
Blue Sky Alpacas Dyed
Cotton (100% organically
grown cotton; 150 yards /
100 grams): 2 hanks #625
Graphite

NEEDLES
One pair straight needles size
US 8 (5 mm)

Change needle size if
necessary to obtain correct
gauge.

NOTIONS
Stitch markers; stitch holders;
two 1" buttons

GAUGE
16 sts and 34 rows = 4" (10 cm)
in Garter stitch (knit every
row)

BODY

CO 88 sts, placing markers after st# 22 and 66. Begin Garter st (knit every row); work even until piece measures 5½" from the beginning.

Separate Fronts and Back

Next Row (RS): K22, BO next st, place last 22 sts worked on st holder for Right Front, k42, BO next st, place last 42 sts worked on separate st holder for Back—22 sts remain.

LEFT FRONT

Working only on Left Front sts, knit to end.

Make Tab (WS): Using Cable CO method (see Special Techniques, page 120), CO 9 sts, knit across CO sts, knit to end—31 sts. Work even for 1 row.

Buttonhole Row (WS): K2, yo, k2tog, knit to end. Work even for 3 rows.

Next Row (WS): BO 9 sts, knit to end—22 sts remain. Work even for 1 row.

Shape Neck (WS): Decrease 1 st at neck edge this row, then every other row 8 times, as follows: K1, k2tog, knit to end—13 sts remain. Work even until piece measures 10½" from the beginning, ending with a WS row. BO all sts.

RIGHT FRONT

With WS facing, rejoin yarn at armhole edge; knit 1 row.

Make Tab (RS): Using Cable CO method, CO 9 sts, knit across CO sts, join another ball of yarn, knit to end—31 sts.

Buttonhole Row (WS): Working both Tab and Front at the same time, using separate balls of yarn, knit to last 4 sts of Tab, k2tog, yo, k2. Work even for 3 rows.

Next Row (WS): Work across all sts, dropping Tab yarn.

Next Row (RS): BO 9 sts, knit to end—22 sts remain.

Complete as for Left Front, reversing neck shaping.

BACK

With WS facing, rejoin yarn to sts on holder for Back. Work even until piece measures 10½" from the beginning, ending with a WS row. BO all sts.

SLEEVES

CO 26 sts. Begin Garter st; work even for 1".

Shape Sleeve (RS): Increase 1 st each side this row, every other row 3 times, then every 4 rows 6 times, as follows: K1, M1, knit to last st, M1, k1—46 sts. Work even until piece measures 5¾" from the beginning, ending with a WS row. BO all sts.

FINISHING

Block pieces to measurements. Sew shoulder seams. Sew in Sleeves. Sew Sleeve seams. Sew on buttons opposite buttonholes. Weave in loose ends.

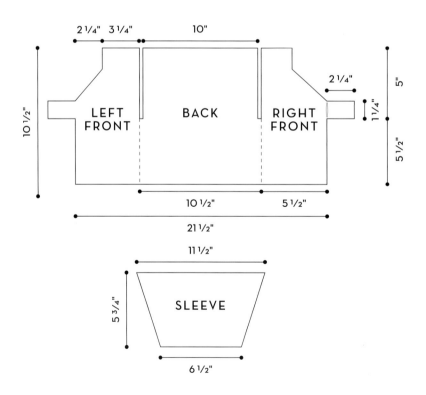

Sadie's Capelet

Easy to knit and, most importantly, simple to slip over baby's head, this cabled coverup is constructed of two rectangular panels sewn together. The optional hood is begun separately, then attached at the neckline.

SIZES
0–3 months, hooded version;
0–6 months, hoodless version

FINISHED
MEASUREMENTS
16" wide at widest point

YARN
Louet Gems Light Worsted
Weight (100% merino wool;
175 yards / 100 grams): 2
hanks #55 Willow (hooded
version), or #47 Terra Cotta
(hoodless version)

NEEDLES
One pair straight needles size
US 8 (5 mm)

One pair straight needles size
US 7 (4.5 mm)

Change needle size if
necessary to obtain correct
gauge.

NOTIONS
Stitch holder; cable needle
(cn)

GAUGE
25 sts and 26 rows = 4"
(10 cm) over st#'s 1–25 of
Panel 1 Chart, using larger
needles.

PANEL 1
Using larger needles, CO 49 sts.

Begin Chart (WS): Work Rows 1–12 of Panel 1 Chart until piece measures approximately 16¾" from the beginning, ending with Row 10 of Chart.

Next Row (WS): Change to smaller needles. Purl 1 row. BO all sts knitwise.

PANEL 2
Using smaller needles, CO 51 sts. Purl 1 row.

Begin Chart (RS): Change to larger needles. Work Rows 1–12 of Panel 2 Chart until piece measures 16¾" from the beginning, ending with Row 3 of Chart. BO all sts in pattern.

PANEL 3 (Hooded Version Only)
Using larger needles, CO 3 sts. Knit 1 row, purl 1 row.

Increase Row: K1, M1, knit to last st, M1, k1—5 sts. Purl 1 row.

Repeat Increase Row every other row 10 times—25 sts. Break yarn and transfer sts to st holder for Hood.

FINISHING
Sew Panels together as indicated in Assembly Diagram on page 48.

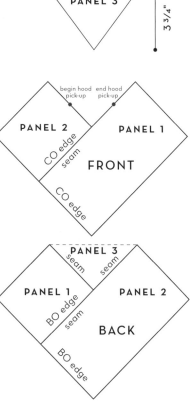

PANELS 1 & 2

16 ³/₄"

7"

4"

PANEL 3

3 ³/₄"

begin hood pick-up   end hood pick-up

PANEL 2   PANEL 1

CO edge
seam

FRONT

CO edge

PANEL 3

seam   seam

PANEL 1   PANEL 2

BO edge
seam

BACK

BO edge

Hood (optional): With RS facing, pick up and knit 13 sts along right neck edge, beginning where indicated in Assembly Diagram, knit across 25 sts from holder for Panel 3, pick up and knit 13 sts along left neck edge, ending where indicated in Assembly Diagram—51 sts.

(WS) K1 (edge st, keep in Garter st [knit every row]), work in Rev St st (knit 1 row, purl 1 row) to last st, k1 (edge st, keep in Garter st). Work even until piece measures 6½" from pick-up row, decrease 1 st on last row—50 sts remain. Divide sts evenly between 2 needles. Using Three-Needle BO (see Special Techniques, page 120), join top of Hood.

Weave in loose ends. Block piece lightly.

PANEL 1 CHART

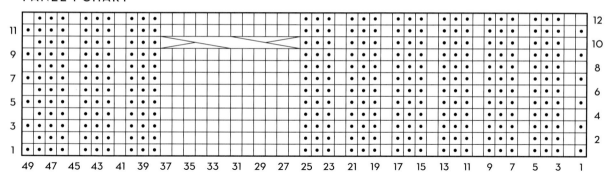

PANEL 2 CHART

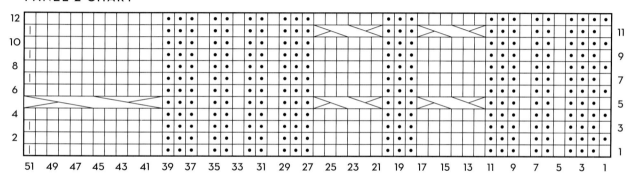

KEY

☐   Knit on RS, purl on WS.

•   Purl on RS, knit on WS.

Ⅰ   Slip 1 knitwise.

⬦   Slip 3 sts to cn, hold to front, k3, k3 from cn.

⬦   Slip 6 sts to cn, hold to front, k6, k6 from cn.

Drawstring Hemp Shorts

These sweet shorts will keep a baby or toddler comfortable during warm weather. The generous sizing and drawstring tie provide plenty of room for growth spurts.

SIZES

3–6 months (6–12 months, 12–18 months, 18–24 months, 2–3 years)

Shown in size 18–24 months

FINISHED MEASUREMENTS

17 ½ (19 ¼, 20, 20 ¾, 22 ½)" waist (without drawstring)

YARN

Lanaknits Allhemp6 (100% hemp; 165 yards / 100 grams): 2 hanks #019 Sprout

NEEDLES

One 16" (40 cm) long circular (circ) needle size US 4 (3.5 mm)

One 16" (40 cm) long circular needle size US 5 (3.75 mm)

One pair straight needles size US 6 (4 mm)

Change needle size if necessary to obtain correct gauge.

NOTIONS

Stitch holder; stitch markers; 28" long ⅜" wide ribbon; safety pin

GAUGE

20 sts and 30 rows = 4" (10 cm) in Stockinette stitch (St st) using size US 5 needle

STITCH PATTERN

3×1 Rib

(multiple of 4 sts + 3; 1-row repeat)

Row 1 (WS): *P3, k1; repeat from * to last 3 sts, p3.

Row 2: Knit the knit sts and purl the purl sts as they face you.

Repeat Row 2 for 3×1 Rib.

LEG

With largest needles, CO 55 (59, 59, 63, 67) sts. Begin 3×1 Rib; work even for 3 rows.

Next Row (RS): Change to size US 5 needle and St st, decrease (decrease, increase, decrease, decrease) 1 st on first row—54 (58, 60, 62, 66) sts. Work even until piece measures 3 (3¼, 3½, 3½, 3¾)" from the beginning, ending with a WS row. Transfer sts to st holder; set aside. Repeat for second Leg; leave sts on needle.

BODY

With RS facing, using size US 5 needle, knit across 27 (29, 30, 31, 33) sts of first Leg from holder, place marker (pm) for side of Leg and beginning of rnd, knit to end of first Leg, knit across 27 (29, 30, 31, 33) sts of second Leg, pm for side of Leg, knit to end—108 (116, 120, 124, 132) sts. Join for working in the rnd; continuing in

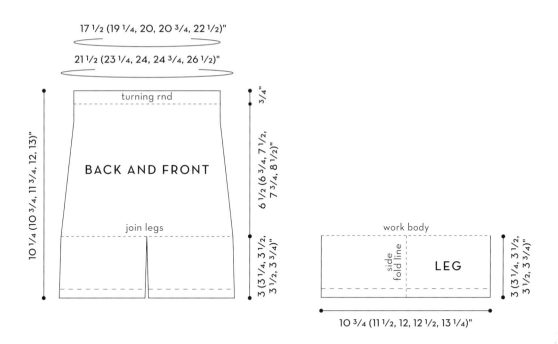

17 1/2 (19 1/4, 20, 20 3/4, 22 1/2)"

21 1/2 (23 1/4, 24, 24 3/4, 26 1/2)"

turning rnd

3/4"

BACK AND FRONT

6 1/2 (6 3/4, 7 1/2, 7 3/4, 8 1/2)"

10 1/4 (10 3/4, 11 3/4, 12, 13)"

join legs

3 (3 1/4, 3 1/2, 3 1/2, 3 3/4)"

work body

side fold line

LEG

3 (3 1/4, 3 1/2, 3 1/2, 3 3/4)"

10 3/4 (11 1/2, 12, 12 1/2, 13 1/4)"

St st (knit every rnd), work even for 9 (11, 13, 15, 17) rnds.

Shape Body: Decrease 4 sts this rnd, then every 7 (7, 8, 8, 9) rnds 4 times, as follows: [K1, ssk, knit to 3 sts before next marker, k2tog, k1, slip marker (sm)] twice—88 (96, 100, 104, 112) sts remain. Work even until piece measures 6 (6 1/4, 7, 7 1/4, 8)" from join.

Eyelet Rnd: K19 (21, 22, 23, 25), ssk, yo, k2, yo, k2tog, knit to end. Work even for 2 rnds. Purl 1 rnd (turning rnd).

Change to size US 4 needle; work even for 3/4" for facing. BO all sts.

FINISHING
Block piece to measurements. Sew inseams. Fold facing over to WS at turning rnd and sew in place, being careful not to let sts show on RS. Slip safety pin through end of ribbon and thread though first eyelet at center front. Push safety pin around waist and out through second eyelet. Trim ribbon to desired length. Weave in loose ends.

Karen's Mohair Kimono

Soft kid mohair creates the perfect wrap for baby's special occasions.

SIZES
0–3 months (3–6 months, 6–12 months)

Shown in size 6–12 months

FINISHED
MEASUREMENTS
13½ (18, 22)" chest

YARN
Nashua Handknits Creative Focus Kid Mohair (75% kid mohair / 20% wool / 5% polyamide; 98 yards / 50 grams): 1 (2, 2) balls #23 Gold

NEEDLES
One pair straight needles size US 10 (6 mm)

One pair double-pointed needles (dpn) size US 8 (5 mm)

Change needle size if necessary to obtain correct gauge.

NOTIONS
Stitch markers; stitch holders

GAUGE
13½ sts and 19 rows = 4" (10 cm) in Stockinette stitch (St st)

STITCH PATTERN

Seed Stitch
(multiple of 2 sts + 1; 1-row repeat)

All Rows: K1, *p1, k1; repeat from * to end.

BODY
Using larger needles, CO 65 (86, 107) sts, placing markers (pm) after st# 21 (28, 35) and 44 (58, 72). Begin Seed st; work even for 3 rows.

Next Row (RS): Work 3 sts in Seed st, work in St st (beginning with a knit row) to last 3 sts, work in Seed st to end.

Work even until piece measures 1¾ (1¾, 2)" from the beginning, ending with a WS row.

Shape Front Neck
Decrease Row 1 (RS): Work 2 sts in Seed st, ssk, knit to last 4 sts, k2tog, work in Seed st to end—63 (84, 105) sts remain.

Decrease Row 2 (WS): Decrease 2 sts this row, then every other row twice, as follows: Work 3 sts in Seed st, p2tog, purl to last 5 sts, p2tog-tbl, work in Seed st to end—57 (78, 99) sts remain. Work even until piece measures 3 (3½, 4)" from the beginning, ending with a WS row.

Separate Fronts and Back (RS): Work 17 (24, 31) sts, transfer remaining 23 (30, 37) sts to first st holder for Back and 17 (24, 31) sts to second st holder for Left Front).

RIGHT FRONT

Size 0-3 Months Only
Shape Neck (WS): Working on Right Front sts only, decrease 1 st at neck edge this row, then every other row 9 times, as follows: Purl to last 5 sts, p2tog-tbl, work in Seed st to end—7 sts remain. Break yarn, leaving a 10-12" tail, and transfer sts to st holder. Set aside.

Sizes 3-6 Months (6-12 Months)

Shape Neck
Decrease Row 1 (WS): Purl to last 5 sts, p2tog-tbl, work in Seed st to end—23 (30) sts remain.

Decrease Row 2: Work 2 sts in Seed st, ssk, work to end—22 (29) sts remain.

Repeat Decrease Rows 1 and 2 three (six) times, then repeat Decrease Row 1 every other row 6 (4) times—10 (13) sts remain. Break yarn, leaving a 10-12" tail, and transfer sts to st holder. Set aside.

LEFT FRONT
Rejoin yarn to sts on holder for Left Front. Work even for 1 row.

Size 0-3 Months Only
Shape Neck (WS): Decrease 1 st at neck edge this row, then every other row 9 times, as follows: Work 3 sts in Seed st, p2tog, work to end—7 sts remain. Break yarn, leaving a 10-12" tail, and transfer sts to st holder. Set aside.

Sizes 3-6 Months (6-12 Months)

Shape Neck
Decrease Row 1 (WS): Work 3 sts in Seed st, p2tog, work to end—23 (30) sts remain.

Decrease Row 2: Work to last 4 sts, k2tog, work to end—22 (29) sts remain.

Repeat Decrease Rows 1 and 2 three (six) times, then repeat Decrease Row 1 every other row 6 (4) times—10 (13) sts remain. Break yarn, leaving a 10-12" tail, and transfer sts to st holder. Set aside.

BACK
Rejoin yarn to sts on holder for Back. Work even in St st until piece measures 7 (7 3/4, 8 3/4)" from the beginning, ending with a RS row.

Work Neck Pattern
Row 1 (WS): P7 (10, 13), work in Seed st to last 7 (10, 13) sts, purl to end. Work even for 2 rows.

Next Row (RS): K7 (10, 13), BO center 9 (10, 11) sts, knit to end. BO remaining sts.

TIES (make 4)
Using dpn, pick up and knit 2 sts at points indicated in schematic. *Note: Three Ties will be picked up from RS, and 1 from WS (see schematic).* Work 2-st I-Cord at each point (see Special Techniques, page 120) until I-Cord measures 6" or desired length.

SLEEVES
Using larger needles, CO 27 sts. Begin Seed st; work even for 3 rows.

Shape Sleeves (RS): Change to St st. Increase 1 st each side this row, then every 4 rows 1 (2, 3) time(s), as follows: K1, M1, work to last st, M1, k1—31 (33, 35) sts. Work even until piece measures 4 (5, 6)". BO all sts.

FINISHING
Block pieces to measurements. Using Three-Needle BO (see Special Techniques, page 120), join shoulder seams. Sew in Sleeves; sew Sleeve seams. Weave in loose ends.

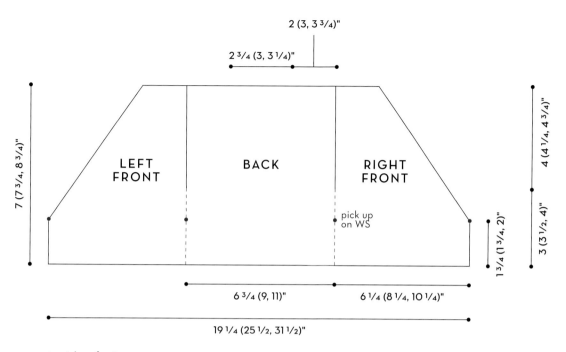

2 (3, 3 3/4)"

2 3/4 (3, 3 1/4)"

LEFT FRONT

BACK

RIGHT FRONT

pick up on WS

7 (7 3/4, 8 3/4)"

4 (4 1/4, 4 3/4)"

3 (3 1/2, 4)"

1 3/4 (1 3/4, 2)"

6 3/4 (9, 11)"

6 1/4 (8 1/4, 10 1/4)"

19 1/4 (25 1/2, 31 1/2)"

● pick up for ties

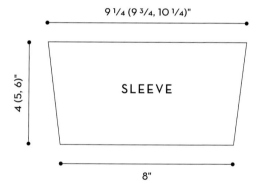

9 1/4 (9 3/4, 10 1/4)"

SLEEVE

4 (5, 6)"

8"

Baby Legwarmers

These soft legwarmers are useful for layering and keeping baby warm when temperatures begin to drop. They're especially handy for babies who squiggle so much that it's hard to put pants on them.

SIZE
6–12 months

FINISHED MEASUREMENTS
8½" circumference × 8¾" long

YARN
Blue Sky Alpacas Skinny Dyed (100% organically grown cotton; 150 yards / 65 grams): 1 hank #304 Zinc

NEEDLES
One set of five double-pointed needles (dpn) size US 5 (3.75 mm)

Change needle size if necessary to obtain correct gauge.

GAUGE
24 sts and 35 rnds = 4" (10 cm) in Stockinette stitch (St st)

STITCH PATTERN

3×1 Rib
(multiple of 4 sts; 1-rnd repeat)

All Rnds: *K3, p1; repeat from * to end.

LEGWARMERS

CO 52 sts. Join for working in the rnd, being careful not to twist sts; place marker (pm) for beginning of rnd. Begin 3×1 Rib; work even until piece measures 1⅝" from the beginning.

Next Rnd: Change to St st (knit every rnd); work even until piece measures 8¾" from the beginning. BO all sts.

FINISHING

Block pieces to measurements. Weave in loose ends.

3 TAKE IT WITH YOU

SIZES
Small (Medium, Large)

FINISHED
MEASUREMENTS
5¼ (8¾, 12¼)" circumference
× 2 (3½, 5¼)" high

YARN
SMALL BAG: **RYC Bamboo Soft**
(100% bamboo; 112 yards /
50 grams): 1 ball #114 Shallot.
*Note: If working with yarn
from your stash, you will need
approximately 14 yards.*

MEDIUM BAG: **Alchemy Yarns
of Transformation Bamboo**
(100% bamboo; 138 yards / 50
grams): 1 hank #65e Dragon.
*Note: If working with yarn
from your stash, you will need
approximately 42 yards.*

LARGE BAG: **Classic Elite Yarns
Soft Linen** (35% wool / 35%
linen / 30% baby alpaca; 137
yards / 50 grams): 1 ball #2285
Cathay. *Note: If working with
yarn from your stash, you will
need approximately 73 yards.*

NEEDLES
One set of five double-pointed
needles (dpn) size US 5 (3.75
mm)

Change needle size if necessary
to obtain correct gauge.

NOTIONS
Stitch marker; 1–2' long ¼"
wide ribbon (optional)

GAUGE
23 sts and 32 rows = 4" (10 cm)
in Stockinette stitch (St st)

Mini Gift Bags

*Whip up one of these gift bags next time you need to wrap a small gift,
such as jewelry, candy, or knitting notions.*

BAG
CO 30 (50, 70) sts, divide among 4 needles [8-8-7-7 (13-13-12-12,
18-18-17-17)]. Join for working in the rnd, being careful not to twist
sts; place marker for beginning of rnd. Begin St st (knit every rnd);
work even for 2 (4, 4) rnds.

Eyelet Rnd: *K3, yo, k2tog; repeat from * to end. Continuing
in St st, work even until piece measures 2 (3½, 5¼)" from the
beginning.

Shape Bottom
Rnd 1: *Slip 1, k1, psso, k2 (6, 10), k2tog; repeat from * to end—20
(40, 60) sts remain.

Rnd 2: *Slip 1, k1, psso, k0 (4, 8), k2tog; repeat from * to end—10
(30, 50) sts remain.

Medium and Large Bags Only
Rnd 3: *Slip 1, k1, psso, k2 (6), k2tog; repeat from * to end—20 (40)
sts remain.

Rnd 4: *Slip 1, k1, psso, k0 (4) k2tog; repeat from * to end—10 (30)
sts remain.

Large Bag Only
Rnd 5: *Slip 1, k1, psso, k2, k2tog; repeat from * to end—20 sts
remain.

Rnd 6: *Slip 1, k1, psso, k2tog; repeat from * to end—10 sts remain.

All Bags

Rnd 3 (5, 7): *K2tog; repeat from * to end—5 sts remain. Break yarn, leaving a long tail. Thread tail through remaining sts, pull tight, and fasten off.

FINISHING

Weave in loose ends.

Drawstring (optional): CO 2 sts. Work 2-st I-Cord (see Special Techniques, page 120) 12 (15, 24)" long, or to desired length.

Thread I-Cord or ribbon through Eyelet Rnd. Tie in a bow.

Summer Satchel

I have knitted many bags, but most of them are wool, so generally more suitable for cool-weather use. I designed this multipurpose bag for the warmer months. I use it to carry produce home from the farmer's market, as a knitting bag, and sometimes as an all-purpose tote.

FINISHED
MEASUREMENTS
24" circumference × 10 1/2"
high, not including handles

YARN
Classic Elite Yarns Provence
(100% mercerized Egyptian
cotton; 205 yards / 100
grams): 2 hanks #2648 Slate
Blue

NEEDLES
One 16" (40 cm) long circular
(circ) needle size US 7 (4.5
mm)

Change needle size if
necessary to obtain correct
gauge.

NOTIONS
Stitch markers; waste yarn;
stitch holder

GAUGE
21 1/2 sts and 28 rows = 4" (10
cm) in Stockinette stitch (St st)

STITCH PATTERN

Fish Scale Lace
(panel of 17 sts; 8-rnd repeat)

Rnd 1: K1, yo, k3, slip 1, k1, psso, p5, k2tog, k3, yo, k1.

Rnd 2: K6, p5, k6.

Rnd 3: K2, yo, k3, slip 1, k1, psso, p3, k2tog, k3, yo, k2.

Rnd 4: K7, p3, k7.

Rnd 5: K3, yo, k3, slip 1, k1, psso, p1, k2tog, k3, yo, k3.

Rnd 6: K8, p1, k8.

Rnd 7: K4, yo, k3, slip 1, k2tog, psso, k3, yo, k4.

Rnd 8: Knit.

Repeat Rnds 1–8 for Fish Scale Lace.

BODY
Using waste yarn, CO 130 sts. Join for working in the rnd, being careful not to twist sts; place marker (pm) for beginning of rnd. Change to working yarn. Begin St st (knit every rnd); work even for 10 rnds.

Begin Pattern: *Work in Fish Scale Lace over 17 sts, pm, k48*, pm for side; repeat from * to *. Work even until 4 vertical repeats of Fish Scale Lace have been worked.

Next Rnd: Change to St st. Work even for 3 rnds.

Eyelet Rnd: [K7, yo, slip 1, k2tog, psso, yo, k7, sm, k48, sm] twice.

Repeat Eyelet Rnd every 8 rnds 3 times. Work even for 3 rnds.

HANDLES
Next Rnd: [K17, sm, k16, BO 16 sts, knit to marker, sm] twice, k33—49 sts remain each handle. Slip sts for second Handle to st holder, removing all markers.

Decrease Row 1 (WS): Working back and forth on first Handle, k1, p2tog, p23, pm, purl to last 3 sts, p2tog-tbl, k1—47 sts remain.

Decrease Row 2 (RS): K1, ssk, knit to last 3 sts, k2tog, k1—45 sts remain.

Repeat Decrease Rows 1 and 2 once, working Eyelets on Decrease Row 2 as follows: K1, ssk, work to marker, sm, yo, slip 1, k2tog, psso, yo, work to last 3 sts, k2tog, k1—41 sts remain.

Continuing to work Eyelets every 8 rows as established, repeat Decrease Rows 1 and 2 seven times—13 sts remain. Work even until Handle measures 9" from BO rnd. Break yarn, leaving 15" tail. Transfer sts to st holder; set aside. Repeat for second Handle. Turn work WS out. Using Three-Needle BO (see Special Techniques, page 120), join Handles.

BOTTOM
Carefully unpick waste yarn from Body sts and place sts on needle—130 sts. Join for working in the rnd.

Shape Bottom
Decrease Rnd 1: K17, pm for beginning of rnd, [ssk, k22, k2tog, pm] 4 times, ssk, k22, k2tog—120 sts remain.

Decrease Rnd 2: *Ssk, knit to 2 sts before marker, k2tog, sm; repeat from * to end—110 sts remain.

Repeat Decrease Rnd 2 every rnd 5 times, every other rnd 3 times, then every rnd twice—10 sts remain.

Decrease Rnd 3: *K2tog; repeat from * to end—5 sts remain.

Break yarn, leaving 8" tail. Thread tail through remaining sts, pull tight, and fasten off.

FINISHING
Weave in loose ends. Block to measurements.

Wickerwork Accessory Bag

For this project, I wanted interesting texture without any fussy stitchwork and I found what I needed when I adapted the Wickerwork stitch pattern from A Second Treasury of Knitting Patterns by Barbara Walker. The fabric lining and zipper closure give the bag a lush and professional-looking finish.

FINISHED MEASUREMENTS
9" wide × 5" high × 2½" deep at base

YARN
Classic Elite Yarns Sundance (50% cotton / 50% microfiber; 83 yards / 50 grams): 2 balls #6288 Salmon

NEEDLES
One 16" (40 cm) long circular (circ) needle size US 7 (4.5 mm)

Change needle size if necessary to obtain correct gauge.

NOTIONS
Stitch markers; 9" zipper; straight pins; sewing needle and thread; 10¼" × 15" piece of fabric, for lining (optional); sewing machine; iron

GAUGE
21 sts and 29 rows = 4" (10 cm) in Wickerwork Pattern

STITCH PATTERN

Wickerwork Pattern
(multiple of 8 sts; 12-rnd repeat)

Rnd 1: K1, *p2, k2; repeat from * to last 3 sts, p2, k1.

Rnd 2: *K1, p1, RT, LT, p1, k1; repeat from * to end.

Rnd 3: *K1, p1, k1, p2, k1, p1, k1; repeat from * to end.

Rnd 4: *K1, RT, p2, LT, k1; repeat from * to end.

Rnd 5: K2, *p4, k4; repeat from * to last 6 sts, p4, k2.

Rnd 6: Knit.

Rnd 7: Repeat Rnd 1.

Rnd 8: *LT, p1, k2, p1, RT; repeat from * to end.

Rnd 9: *P1, k1, p1, k2, p1, k1, p1; repeat from * to end.

Rnd 10: *P1, LT, k2, RT, p1; repeat from * to end.

Rnd 11: P2, *k4, p4; repeat from * to last 6 sts, k4, p2.

Rnd 12: Knit.

Repeat Rnds 1–12 for Wickerwork Pattern.

ABBREVIATIONS

RT: Skip first st, knit second st, leaving st on needle, knit first st, slip both sts from needle together.

LT: Skip first st, knit into back of second st, leaving st on needle, knit into front of first st, slip both sts from needle together.

BOTTOM

CO 116 sts. Join for working in the rnd, being careful not to twist sts; place marker (pm) for beginning of rnd, and after st# 10, 58, and 68. Purl 3 rnds.

BODY

Begin Pattern: [Knit to marker, slip marker (sm), work in Wickerwork Pattern to next marker, sm] twice. Work even for 7 rnds.

Decrease Rnd: Ssk, knit to 2 sts before marker, k2tog, sm, work to next marker, sm, ssk, knit to 2 sts before marker, k2tog, work to end—112 sts remain. Work even for 9 rnds.

Repeat Decrease Rnd once—108 sts remain. Work even for 7 rnds.

Repeat Decrease Rnd once—104 sts remain. Work even for 7 rnds.

Repeat Decrease Rnd once—100 sts remain. Work even for 1 rnd. BO all sts purlwise.

FINISHING

Sew bottom seam. Weave in loose ends. Block piece to measurements. Sew in zipper as follows: Turn Bag WS out. Position zipper along open top of bag and pin into place on WS. Using sewing needle and thread, baste outer edge of zipper to Bag from WS (see Special Techniques, page 120). Turn bag RS out. Using Invisible st (see Special Techniques, page 120), sew zipper to edge of Bag.

Lining (optional): Fold fabric in half lengthwise so that RS's are together. Secure with straight pins. Using sewing needle and thread or sewing machine, sew side edges, using ½" seam allowance. Sew lining gusset seams (see diagram). Using warm iron, press seams flat. Fold top edge of lining over ½" to WS and press. Insert completed lining into Bag so that WS's of lining and Bag are together. Using sewing needle and thread, and Invisible st, sew lining to WS of Bag.

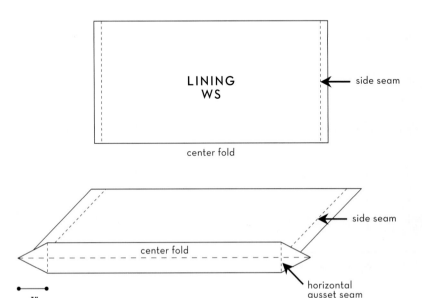

LINING WS

side seam

center fold

side seam

center fold

horizontal gusset seam

1"

Felted Bag

Nickel rings and a chain handle give this traditional bag an updated look. The outside pocket is a handy place to store keys, a cell phone, or anything else to which you need easy access.

FINISHED MEASUREMENTS
14 ¾" wide at widest point × 15" high, before felting

12 ½" wide × 10" high, after felting

Note: Results will depend on felting conditions and time spent felting.

YARN
Louet Riverstone Chunky Weight (100% wool; 165 yards / 100 grams): 2 hanks #42 Eggplant

NEEDLES
One 24" (60 cm) long circular (circ) needle size US 11 (8 mm)

Change needle size if necessary to obtain correct gauge.

NOTIONS
Stitch holders; stitch markers; cotton waste yarn; sharp tapestry needle; embroidery floss; 1 yard linen or topstitching thread in matching color; 24" chain; two 1½" silver rings that open and close; one 2" closed nickel or silver ring (see Sources for Supplies on page 124 for all bag hardware)

GAUGE
13 sts and 17 rows = 4" (10 cm) in Stockinette stitch (St st)

POCKET LINING
CO 24 sts. Begin St st; work even until piece measures 8" from the beginning, ending with a WS row. Break yarn and transfer sts to st holder.

BODY
CO 96 sts. Join for working in the rnd, being careful not to twist sts; place marker (pm) for beginning of rnd, and after st# 48. Begin St st; work even until piece measures 9" from the beginning.

Shape Body: [K1, ssk, knit to 3 sts before marker, k2tog, k1, slip marker (sm)] twice—92 sts remain. Work even for 8 rnds.

Join Pocket Lining: K11, BO 24 sts, knit to marker, sm, knit to end.

Next Rnd: K1, ssk, k8, knit across Pocket Lining sts from holder, k8, k2tog, k1, sm, k1, ssk, knit to 3 sts before marker, k2tog, k1—88 sts remain. Work even for 8 rnds.

Next Rnd: [K1, ssk] twice, work to 6 sts before marker, [k1, k2tog] twice, sm, knit to end—84 sts remain (40 sts for back, 44 sts for front). Work even for 2 rnds.

Next Rnd: Knit to marker, sm, k4, BO 36 sts, knit to end—48 sts remain.

Next Row (RS): Knit to marker, remove marker, transfer next 4 sts to st holder for Tab.

Next Row (WS): Purl to marker, remove marker, transfer next 4 sts to st holder for Tab—40 sts remain.

FLAP

Next Row: Continuing in St st, work even for 11 rows.

Shape Flap (RS): K1, [ssk] twice, knit to last 5 sts, [k2tog] twice, k1—36 sts remain. Work even for 3 rows.

Repeat last 4 rows once—32 sts remain.

Next Row: K1, [ssk] 3 times, knit to last 7 sts, [k2tog] 3 times, k1—26 sts remain. Work even for 3 rows. BO all sts. Break yarn. Weave in loose ends.

TABS

Rejoin yarn to sts on holder for Tab. Begin St st; work even until piece measures 4". BO all sts. Break yarn. Weave in loose ends. Repeat for opposite Tab.

FINISHING

Sew bottom seam. Turn bag WS out and flatten bottom. Sew a short seam across the triangular flap at each side, approximately 1½" from end of each triangle point, to form bottom and side gussets for bag (see diagram). With WS of Bag facing, sew Pocket Lining to Back, being careful not to let sts show on RS.

Using cotton waste yarn and ½" sts, loosely baste top of Pocket to Pocket Lining, and Flap to front of Bag (see Special Techniques, page 120). *Note: This keeps the openings from flaring and helps preserve the Flap shaping during the felting process. Keep a very close eye on these two sections while felting; overfelting may cause the pieces to felt together. If the areas begin to felt together, gently pull them apart.*

Felting: Felt Bag to desired dimensions (see Special Techniques, page 120). Allow Bag to air-dry completely. Remove waste yarn from Flap and Pocket. Using tapestry needle, full strand of embroidery floss, and Satin st (see Special Techniques, page 120), sew large ring to bottom center of Flap (see photo).

Open 1 jump ring (see Special Techniques, page 120), slip ring through 1 end of chain; close ring. Repeat for opposite end. *Note: Be prepared to use some muscle—rings of this size and thickness will take some effort to open and close.*

Insert felted Tab through jump ring and sew end of Tab to WS of Bag using tapestry needle and linen or topstitching thread. Repeat for opposite Tab.

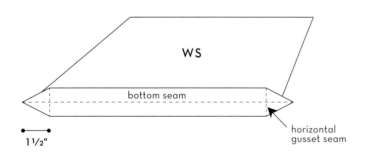

WS

bottom seam

1½"

horizontal gusset seam

Silk Gelato Clutch

For this clutch, I combined the Silk Gelato fabric yarn I developed with Lantern Moon and Muench's Touch Me chenille. I love the way the flat Gelato and roundish, slippery Touch Me complement each other and how the herringbone stitch pattern gives the knitted fabric a woven appearance.

FINISHED MEASUREMENTS
10" wide × 6" high

YARN
Leigh Radford / Lantern Moon Silk Gelato (100% silk; 72 yards / 100 grams): 1 ball Vanilla Bean

Muench Yarns Touch Me (72% rayon microfiber / 28% new wool; 61 yards / 50 grams): 1 ball #3617

NEEDLES
One 16" (40 cm) long circular (circ) needle size US 35 (19 mm)

One spare needle size US 35 (19 mm) for BO

Change needle size if necessary to obtain correct gauge.

NOTIONS
Removable stitch marker; 10" straight hex-open frame (see Sources for Supplies, page 124); 10 1/2" × 15" piece of fabric, for lining; straight pins; sewing needle and thread; sewing machine; iron

GAUGE
2 1/4 sts and 8 rnds = 4" (10 cm) in Twist Stitch pattern using 1 strand of each yarn held together

STITCH PATTERN

Twist Stitch Pattern
(multiple of 2 sts; 2-rnd repeat)

Rnd 1: *K2tog-tbl, slipping first st off needle and leaving second st on needle; repeat from * to end, working last st of rnd together with first st of next rnd.

Rnd 2: *K2tog, slipping first st off needle and leaving second st on needle; repeat from * to end, working last st of rnd together with first st of next rnd.

Repeat Rnds 1 and 2 for Twist Stitch Pattern.

BODY

Using one strand of each yarn held together, CO 46 sts very loosely. Join for working in the rnd, being careful not to twist sts; place removable marker on first st for beginning of rnd. Begin Twist Stitch Pattern; work even until piece measures 6" from the beginning, ending with Rnd 1.

FINISHING

Turn work inside out. Remove marker and slip 23 sts to a spare needle. Using Three-Needle BO (see Special Techniques, page 120), BO all sts. Weave in loose ends.

Lining: Fold fabric in half lengthwise so that RS's are together. Secure sides with straight pins. Using sewing needle and thread or sewing machine, sew side edges, using ½" seam allowance. Using warm iron, press seams flat. Fold top edge of lining over ¼" to WS and press. Slip lining through spring frame. Fold fabric over frame 1¾" so that WS's are together. Using sewing needle and thread, and Invisible st (see Special Techniques, page 120), sew folded fabric to body of lining. Insert completed lining into Clutch so that WS's are together; pin lining into place. Using sewing needle and thread, and Invisible st, sew lining to WS of Clutch.

FINISHED MEASUREMENTS
15 ¾" wide × 9 ¾" high × 3 ¼" deep, before felting

Approximately 14 ½" wide × 6" high × 2 ½" deep, after felting

Note: Results will depend on felting conditions and time spent felting.

YARN
Ella Rae Classic (100% wool; 220 yards / 100 grams): 1 skein each #108 Mustard Heather (MC) and #104 Silver Heather (A)

NEEDLES
One pair straight needles size US 10 ½ (6.5 mm)

Change needle size if necessary to obtain correct gauge.

NOTIONS
Stitch markers; 1 magnetic closure; two 1" wide UMX Easy-Open-Easy-Lock Purse Hooks (sometimes called handle clips); two 18 ½" chains; 2 pair small pliers; sharp tapestry needle; 1 yard linen or topstitching thread; 15" × 17" piece of fabric, for lining; straight pins; sewing needle and thread; sewing machine; iron (see Sources for Supplies, page 124, for all bag hardware)

GAUGE
16 sts and 24 rows = 4" (10 cm) in Stockinette stitch (St st)

Connected Squares Felted Handbag

I created the motif for this bag by sketching squares in a variety of sizes, then moving them around until I settled on the composition you see here. The chain handle and velvet lining give this piece a fancy appeal.

BAG

INTARSIA PANEL (make 2)
Using MC, CO 63 sts. Begin pattern from Chart. Work even, changing colors as indicated, until entire Chart is complete. BO all sts.

GUSSET
Using MC, CO 7 sts. Begin St st. Work even until piece measures 7 ¾" from the beginning, ending with a WS row.

Shape Gusset
Increase Row (RS): K1, k1-f/b, knit to last 2 sts, k1-f/b, k1—9 sts. Work even for 3 ½", ending with a WS row. Repeat from * twice—13 sts. Work even for 12", ending with a WS row.

Decrease Row (RS): K1, ssk, knit to last 3 sts, k2tog, k1—11 sts. Work even for 3 ½", ending with a WS row. Repeat from * twice—7 sts remain. Work even for 4 ¼", ending with a WS row. BO all sts.

FINISHING
Sew Gusset to Intarsia Panels, sewing CO edge of each Intarsia Panel to long center work-even portion of sides of Gusset. Sew shaped edges of Gusset to side edges of Intarsia Panels, leaving approximately 5" of each end of Gusset unsewn. Weave in loose ends.

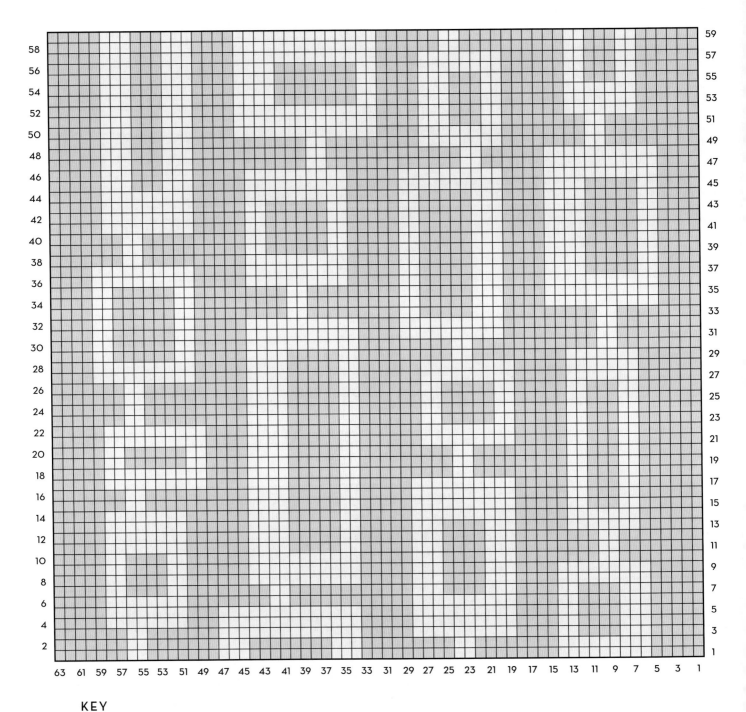

KEY

□ Knit on RS, purl on WS.　　▨ MC　　□ A

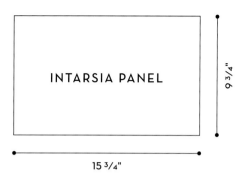

INTARSIA PANEL

9 3/4"

15 3/4"

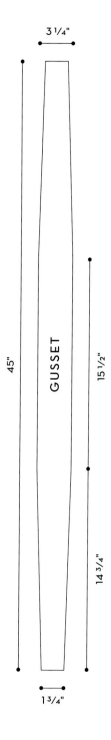

3 1/4"

45"

GUSSET

15 1/2"

14 3/4"

1 3/4"

Felting: Felt Bag to desired dimensions (see Special Techniques, page 120).

Purse Hooks: Insert 1 end of Gusset through purse hook and sew edge of Gusset to WS of Bag using tapestry needle and linen or topstitching thread. *Note: I like to use linen to sew Gusset ends in place as it provides a very strong attachment. Topstitching or heavy-duty sewing thread is a good alternative if you don't have linen.* Repeat for opposite side.

Handle: Attach last open link in chain to purse hook (see Jump Rings, Special Techniques, page 120). Repeat for second chain on same purse hook, then repeat for both chains on opposite side.

Lining: Fold fabric in half lengthwise so that RS's are together. Secure with straight pins. Using sewing needle and thread or sewing machine, sew side edges, using 1/2" seam allowance. Sew lining gusset seams (see diagram on page 82). Using warm iron, press seams flat. Fold top edge of lining over ½" to WS and press. Following manufacturer's instructions, attach magnetic closures to center of top edge, approximately 1¼" down from top. Insert lining into Bag so that WS's of lining and Bag are together; pin lining into place. Using sewing needle and thread, and Invisible st (see Special Techniques, page 120), sew lining to WS of Bag.

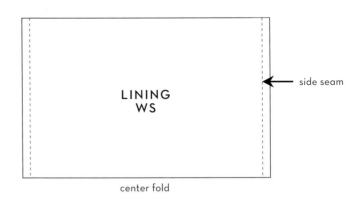

LINING
WS

side seam

center fold

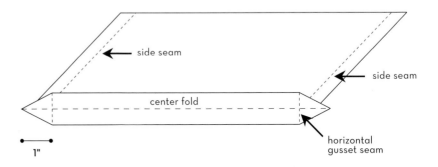

side seam

side seam

center fold

horizontal
gusset seam

1"

MAKE YOUR HOUSE
A HOME

Bastille's Ball

These felted balls are among my cat Bastille's favorite toys to bat around the house; they also give me something to do with leftover scraps of yarn. For variety, change the length of the I-cord spikes, insert a bell prior to felting, or leave a small opening on the outside, then after the felting is finished and the ball is dry, tuck some catnip into it.

FINISHED MEASUREMENTS

4 ¼" wide at widest point × 5" high, before felting and adding Spikes, laid flat

Approximately 5 ½" circumference, including Spikes, after felting

Note: Results will depend on felting conditions and time spent felting.

YARN

Manos del Uruguay Classic Wool (100% wool; 138 yards / 100 grams): 1 hank #26 Rosin, #40 Goldenrod, or #U Rust. *Note: If working with yarn from your stash, you will need approximately 22 yards worsted-weight 100% non-machine-washable wool.*

NEEDLES

One set of five double-pointed needles (dpn) size US 10 ½ (6.5 mm)

NOTIONS

Stitch marker; 2 tbsp. dried catnip (optional); 18 mm or larger jingle bell (optional—see Sources for Supplies, page 124; note that a smaller bell may fall out during felting); sewing needle and matching thread (optional)

GAUGE

12 sts and 16 rows = 4" (10 cm) in Stockinette stitch (St st)

Note: Gauge not critical for this project.

BODY

CO 12 sts, leaving a 12" tail. Join for working in the rnd, being careful not to twist sts; place marker (pm) for beginning of rnd.

Rnds 1 and 2: Knit.

Rnd 3: *K1, k1-f/b; repeat from * to end—18 sts.

Rnds 4 and 5: Knit.

Rnd 6: *K1, k1-f/b; repeat from * to last 2 sts, k2—27 sts.

Rnds 7-13: Knit.

Rnd 14: *K1, k2tog, k1, ssk; repeat from * to last 2 sts, k3—18 sts remain.

Rnds 15 and 16: Knit.

Rnd 17: *K1, k2tog, k1, ssk; repeat from * to end—12 sts remain.

Rnds 18-20: Knit.

Break yarn, leaving a 4" tail. Thread tail through remaining sts; pull tight and fasten off. Weave in loose ends.

SPIKES (make 20)

With dpn, pick up and knit 3 sts from surface of Ball. Work I-Cord (see Special Techniques, page 120) for 3 rows.

Next Row: K3tog–1 st remains. Break yarn, leaving a 3" tail. Fasten off remaining st. Weave tail into I-Cord. Repeat for remaining Spikes, making sure to space them evenly. Weave in loose ends.

FINISHING

Insert bell (optional); sew CO edge closed. If you plan to stuff Ball with catnip, leave CO edge open and weave in tail prior to felting.

Felting: Felt Ball to desired dimensions (see Special Techniques, page 120). As the felting process progresses, the opening at the CO edge will begin to close. Keep an eye on this area throughout the felting process. If you've inserted a jingle bell, make sure the bell hasn't fallen out through the opening. If it has, reinsert it and let the felting process resume–the bell size

called for is large enough that it shouldn't easily fall out, but with the agitation of the felting cycle, some bells do work themselves free. If you plan on stuffing the Ball with catnip, make sure the opening remains large enough to insert it once the Ball is felted and dry. If the opening looks like it's closing up, stretch it during the felting process and it will remain large enough for you to insert the catnip.

Once the Ball is felted, set it aside to air-dry. Use your fingers to position the Spikes as desired. If you'd like them to lay closer to the surface, roll the felted Ball in your hand. This will cause the Spikes to lay flatter. Let dry completely. Insert desired amount of dry catnip into opening (optional). With sewing needle and thread, sew opening closed.

Hot-Water Bottle Cover

Whether you need to soothe aching muscles or take the chill off a cold winter's night, this cozy hot-water bottle cover is sure to please.

FINISHED MEASUREMENTS
8" wide × 13" long, including neck

YARN
Brown Sheep Company Lamb's Pride Bulky (85% wool / 15% mohair; 125 yards / 4 ounces): 1 skein #M176 Silver Gray

NEEDLES
One set of five double-pointed needles (dpn) size US 9 (5.5 mm)

One set of five double-pointed needles size US 11 (8 mm)

One 16" (40 cm) circular (circ) needle size US 11 (8 mm)

Change needle size if necessary to obtain correct gauge.

NOTIONS
Stitch markers; stitch holders

GAUGE
11 sts and 19 rows = 4" (10 cm) in Seed stitch, using larger needles

STITCH PATTERN

Seed Stitch
(multiple of 2 sts; 1-rnd repeat)

Rnd 1: *K1, p1; repeat from * to end.

Rnd 2: Knit the purl sts and purl the knit sts as they face you.

Repeat Rnd 2 for Seed Stitch.

BODY
Using circ needle, CO 44 sts. Join for working in the rnd, being careful not to twist sts; place marker (pm) for beginning of rnd and after st# 22. Begin Seed st; work even until piece measures 11" from the beginning, or to fit length of water bottle to base of neck.

Shape Neck: BO 7 sts, k8 (including last st on right-hand needle), BO next 14 sts, k8 (including last st on right-hand needle), BO last 7 sts. Break yarn, leaving 10" tail.

Transfer each section of 8 sts to st holders. Sew BO edges together. Transfer sts from st holders to smaller dpns; pick up and knit 2 sts in each seam—20 sts. Join for working in the rnd. Continuing in Seed st, work even for 1". Change to larger dpns; work even for 1". BO all sts in pattern.

FINISHING
Weave in loose ends. Block to measurements.

Heated Lavender Pillow

I have a row of lavender growing alongside my driveway. To contain its fragrance so I can enjoy it year-round, I dried some and mixed it with rice in a muslin bag, then placed the bag inside this knitted cotton-silk sleeve. Now, whenever I want to revive the lavender's soothing scent and relax sore muscles, I just pop the whole package into the microwave for a couple of minutes.

FINISHED MEASUREMENTS
9 1/2" wide × 8 1/2" long

Note: Because of the bulk of the knitted fabric, approximately 1/4" of fabric will be taken up in each fold.

YARN
Misti International Pima Cotton & Silk (83% Peruvian pima cotton / 17% silk; 191 yards / 100 grams): 1 hank #6208 Sunshine

NEEDLES
One pair straight needles size US 8 (5 mm)

One pair double-pointed needles (dpn) size US 8 (5 mm)

Change needle size if necessary to obtain correct gauge.

NOTIONS
Tapestry needle; 10 1/2" × 18" piece of cotton muslin or other thin fabric, for lining; straight pins; sewing needle and thread or sewing machine; 4 – 4 1/2 cups long grain rice; approximately 1 tbsp. dried lavender; one 1" button (not metal)

GAUGE
19 sts and 27 rows = 4" (10 cm) in Stockinette stitch (St st)

STITCH PATTERN

Garter Lace
(multiple of 4 sts; 1-row repeat)

All Rows: K3, *yo, p2tog, k2; repeat from * to last st, k1.

PILLOW
Using straight needles, CO 44 sts. Begin Garter Lace; work even until piece measures 15 3/4" from the beginning.

Next Row (RS): K3, *k2tog, M1, k2; repeat from * to last st, k1.

Next Row: Change to St st, beginning with a purl row. Work even until piece measures 20 1/2" from the beginning, ending with a RS row. Break yarn, leaving 6" tail.

FINISHING
I-Cord Trim: Turn work so WS is facing you. Using dpn, CO 2 sts. Work Applied I-Cord (see Special Techniques, page 120) across 22 sts, work free I-Cord for 1 3/4" for button loop, work Applied I-Cord across last 22 sts. Break yarn, leaving 18" tail. Thread tapestry needle with tail and work Running st (see Special Techniques, page 120) back through top of I-Cord to stabilize I-Cord and

prevent edge of piece from rolling.

Block to measurements. Lay piece flat with WS facing you. Fold front up at 6¾" and flap down at beginning of St st, overlapping flap over front by 2" (see schematic). Sew side seams, sewing side edges of flap into seam. Weave in loose ends. Sew button opposite button loop.

Fabric Insert: Fold fabric in half lengthwise so that RS's are together. Secure with straight pins. With sewing needle and thread or sewing machine, sew around open edges, using ½" seam allowance, and leaving opening at one corner to pour in rice. Turn Pillow RS out. Mix rice and lavender and pour into opening. Sew opening closed. *Note: I have found that 1 tablespoon of lavender is plenty, but you can adjust the amount as desired. Once the Pillow is heated, the lavender aroma really comes through.*

Place Fabric Insert in Pillow. Heat in microwave for 2 to 3 minutes. Place on tired muscles and relax.

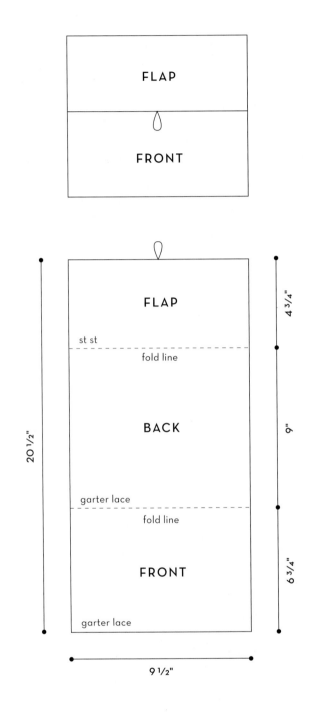

Pencil Sketch Washcloths & Mitt

I felt like I was using my knitting needles as drawing pencils when I worked out the lines and circles in this washcloth and mitt set. I chose a mercerized cotton yarn with a nice sheen because it shows off the stitch pattern clearly and is also soft and absorbent.

FINISHED MEASUREMENTS

WASHCLOTHS: 9¼" wide × 8" high

BATH MITT: 6½" square

YARN

ONLine Linie 12 Clip (100% mercerized Egyptian mako cotton; 182 yards / 100 grams):
WASHCLOTHS: 1 hank #190 Pearly Green. *Note: One hank makes 2 Washcloths.*
BATH MITT: 1 hank #44 Oatmeal

NEEDLES

One pair double-pointed needles (dpn) size US 6 (4 mm)

One pair double-pointed needles size US 7 (4.5 mm)

Change needle size if necessary to obtain correct gauge.

NOTIONS

Cable needle (cn); stitch markers

GAUGE

WASHCLOTHS: 24 sts and 28 rows = 4" (10 cm) in Stockinette stitch (St st), using smaller needles

BATH MITT: 24 sts and 31 rows = 4" (10 cm) in Cable Pattern from Chart A, using larger needles

WASHCLOTHS

Using larger needles, CO 64 sts. Begin pattern from Chart B or C. Work even for 3 rows. Change to smaller needles. Work even until Row 53 is complete. Change to larger needles. Work even until Chart is complete. BO all sts in pattern.

FINISHING

Weave in loose ends. Block to measurements.

MITT

Using larger needles, CO 78 sts. Join for working in the rnd, being careful not to twist sts; place marker (pm) for beginning of rnd, and after st# 39. Begin Chart A; work Rnds 1–3. Change to smaller needles. Work even until entire Chart is complete.

FINISHING

Divide sts evenly onto 2 needles. Carefully turn work inside out so that WS is facing you. Join sts using Three-Needle BO (see Special Techniques, page 120).

Weave in loose ends.

CHART A

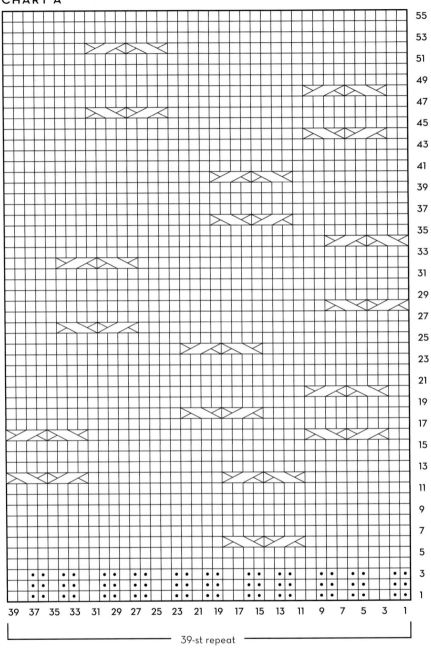

55
53
51
49
47
45
43
41
39
37
35
33
31
29
27
25
23
21
19
17
15
13
11
9
7
5
3
1

39 37 35 33 31 29 27 25 23 21 19 17 15 13 11 9 7 5 3 1

⊢———————————— 39-st repeat ————————————⊣

KEY

☐ Knit

⊡ Purl

▱ Slip 2 sts to cn, hold to back, k2, k2 from cn.

▱ Slip 2 sts to cn, hold to front, k2, k2 from cn.

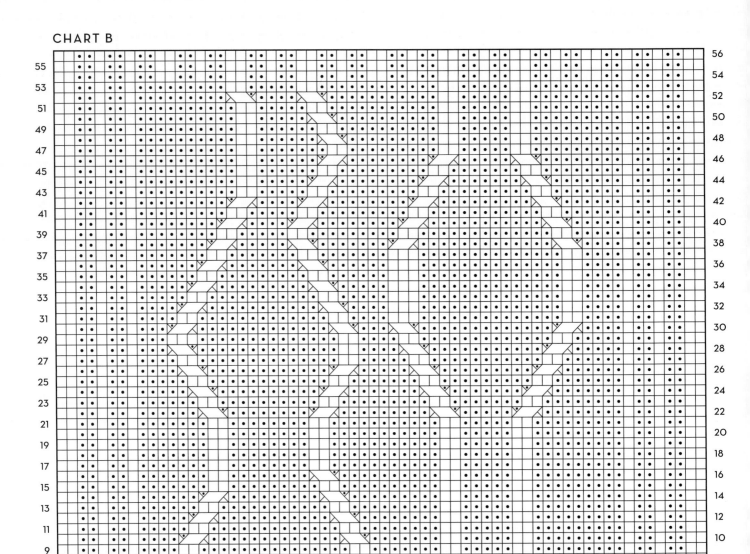

CHART C

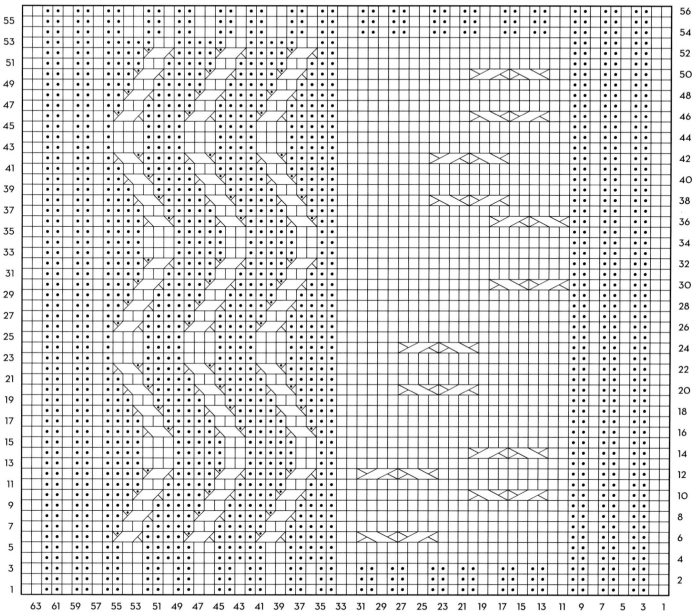

KEY

☐ Knit on RS, purl on WS.

• Purl on RS, knit on WS.

 Slip 1 st to cn, hold to back, k2, p1 from cn.

Slip 2 sts to cn, hold to front, p1, k2 from cn.

Slip 2 sts to cn, hold to back, k2, k2 from cn.

Slip 2 sts to cn, hold to front, k2, k2 from cn.

Albers Stash Blanket

Named after the acclaimed abstract painter and theorist Josef Albers, this beautiful blanket—worked in individual panels in a reversible rib pattern—is a good way to use partial skeins of yarn in a similar gauge leftover from other projects. Do all of the knitting yourself, or make it a group project with each member contributing a panel.

FINISHED MEASUREMENTS

PANELS: **4" wide × 56" long,** before blocking

7 ¼" wide × 73" long, after blocking

BLANKET: **66" × 73",** after blocking

YARN

Worsted-weight yarn; 36-row block weighs approximately 9 ounces; 12-row block weighs approximately 4 ounces. *Note: Weight and yardage can vary from one yarn to the next; be sure to have more yarn than is listed for each block.*

NEEDLES

One pair straight needles size US 10 (6 mm)

Change needle size if necessary to obtain correct gauge.

NOTIONS

Kitchen scale

GAUGE

44 sts and 36 rows = 4" (10 cm) in Rib Pattern A, before blocking

STITCH PATTERNS

Rib Pattern A (Panel 1)

(multiple of 6 sts; 1-row repeat)

Row 1 (WS): P5, *k2, p4; repeat from * to last st, p1.

Row 2: Knit the knit sts and purl the purl sts as they face you.

Repeat Row 2 for Rib Pattern A.

Rib Pattern B (Panels 2-9)

(multiple of 6 sts + 8; 1-row repeat)

Row 1 (WS): P5, *k2, p4; repeat from * to last st, k3.

Row 2: Knit the knit sts and purl the purl sts as they face you.

Repeat Row 2 for Rib Pattern B.

BLANKET

Note: You may choose your own color pattern, or follow the Color Map for color changes. After completing each color and adding a new color, leave 8" tails. You may use these tails for sewing Panels together.

Panel 1

CO 42 sts. Begin Rib Pattern A; *work even for 36 rows. Change to new color; work even for 12 rows. Repeat from * 6 times. BO all sts in pattern.

Panels 2, 4, 6, and 8

CO 44 sts. Begin Rib Pattern B; work even for 12 rows. *Change to new color; work even for 12 rows. Change to new color; work even for 36 rows. Repeat from * 5 times. Change to new color; work even for 12 rows. Change to new color; work even for 24 rows. BO all sts in pattern.

Panels 3, 5, 7, and 9

CO 44 sts. Begin Rib Pattern B; *work even for 36 rows. Change to new color; work even for 12 rows. Repeat from * 6 times. BO all sts in pattern.

FINISHING

Block each Panel to measurements. With RS facing, using Mattress st (see Special Techniques, page 120) and tails (or yarn of choice), sew Panels together, making sure Panel 1 is at right-hand edge and Panel 9 is at left-hand edge, with Panels in order in between, and with all CO edges at same end.

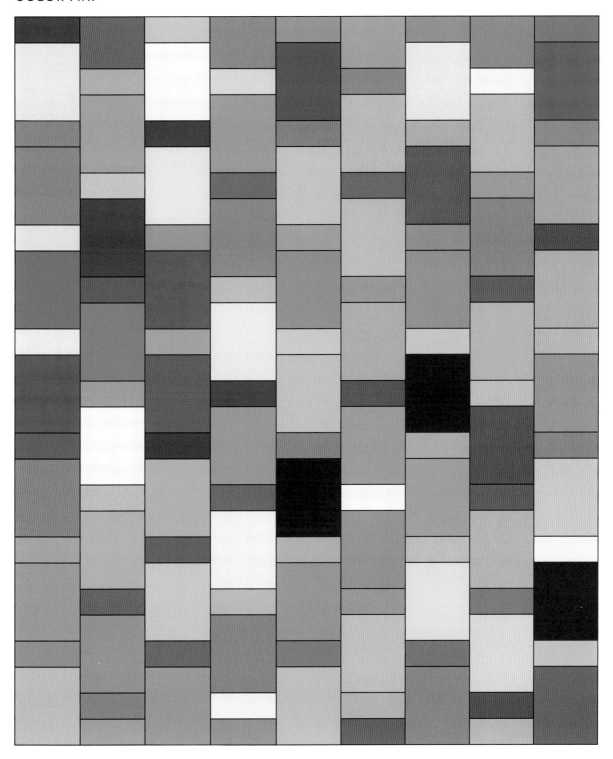

SHOWN LEFT TO RIGHT:
LITTLE BOXES, HALF-AND-HALF, BASIC

YARN
Brown Sheep Company Lamb's
Pride Bulky (85% wool / 15%
mohair; 125 yards / 4 ounces):
2 skeins each pillow (either
size) #M28 Chianti (A, Basic
Pillow), #M18 Khaki (B, Half-
and-Half Pillow), or #M83
Raspberry (C, Little Boxes
Pillow)

NEEDLES
One 24" (60 cm) long circular
(circ) needle size US 9
(5.5 mm)

One 24" (60 cm) long circular
needle size US 10½ (6.5 mm)

One spare needle size
US 10½ (6.5 mm) for BO

Change needle size if
necessary to obtain correct
gauge.

NOTIONS
Stitch markers; four 1–1¼"
buttons each pillow; 12" or
14" pillow form, depending on
size worked; Note: Make sure
stitch markers do not create
gap between stitches; use
removable stitch markers if
necessary.

GAUGE
13 sts and 19 rows = 4" (10 cm)
in Stockinette stitch (St st),
using larger needle

Basic Pillows

A perfect beginner project, this trio of pillows is simple and quick to knit.

BASIC PILLOW

Button Band

Using smaller needle and A, CO 82 (94) sts. Join for working in the rnd, being careful not to twist sts; place marker (pm) for beginning of rnd and after st# 41 (47). Begin Garter st (knit 1 rnd, purl 1 rnd); work even for 4 rnds.

Buttonhole Rnd: K7 (10), [BO 3 sts, k5] 3 times, BO 3 sts, knit to marker, slip marker (sm), knit to end. Work even for 1 rnd, CO 3 sts over BO sts. Work even in Garter st for 4 rnds.

Body

Change to larger needle and St st; work even until piece measures 13¼ (15¼)" from the beginning.

FINISHING

Turn work inside out. Remove markers and slip 41 (47) sts to a spare needle. Using Three-Needle BO (see Special Techniques, page 120), BO all sts. Weave in loose ends. Sew buttons opposite buttonholes. Insert pillow form.

HALF-AND-HALF PILLOW

Using B, work as for Basic Pillow through Button Band.

Body

Change to larger needle and St st. Work even until piece measures 5¾ (6¾)" from the beginning. Change to Rev St st (purl every rnd); work even until piece measures 13¼ (15¼)" from the beginning. Complete as for Basic Pillow, binding off all sts purlwise instead of knitwise.

LITTLE BOXES PILLOW

Using C, work as for Basic Pillow through Button Band.

Body

Change to larger needle.

Rnds 1–4 (5): Knit.

Rnd 5 (6): *K1 (2), [p3, k9 (7)] 3 (4) times, p3, k1 (2), slip marker (sm); rep from * to end.

Rnd 6 (7): Knit.

Rnd 7 (8): Repeat Rnd 5 (6).

Rnds 8 (9)–18 (22): Knit.

Rnd 19 (23): *K7, [p3, k9 (7)] 2 (3) times, p3, k7, sm; repeat from * to end.

Rnd 20 (24): Knit.

Rnd 21 (25): Repeat Rnd 19 (23).

Rnds 22 (26)–31 (39): Knit.

Repeat Rnds 5–21 (6–25) once. Change to St st (knit every rnd); work even until piece measures 13½ (15¼)" from the beginning. Complete as for Basic Pillow.

HALF-AND-HALF

Pleated Vase Sleeve

This felted sleeve is a simple way to dress up a plain vase. It also protects the tabletop from scratches and small water spills. After knitting and felting, the wet sleeve is slipped over the vase, then gently pleated. The pleats are held in place with U or T pins until they dry.

FINISHED MEASUREMENTS

13 ¼" circumference × 22½" high, before felting

12" circumference × 10 ¾" high, after felting and pleating

Note: Results will depend on felting conditions and time spent felting.

YARN

Berroco Ultra Alpaca (50% superfine alpaca / 50% Peruvian highland wool; 215 yards / 100 grams): 1 hank #6280 Mahogany Mix

NEEDLES

One set of five double-pointed needles (dpn) size US 10 ½ (6.5 mm)

One 16" (40 cm) long circular (circ) needle size US 10 ½ (6.5 mm)

Change needle size if necessary to obtain correct gauge.

NOTIONS

Stitch markers; U or T pins; glass vase, 12" circumference × 10 ¾" high

GAUGE

15 sts and 22 rows = 4" (10 cm) in Stockinette stitch (St st), before felting

SLEEVE

Note: Change to circ needle when appropriate for number of sts on needle.

Using dpns, CO 41 sts. Join for working in the rnd, being careful not to twist sts; place marker (pm) for beginning of rnd. Purl 1 rnd, knit 1 rnd, purl 1 rnd.

Next Rnd: Begin St st (knit every rnd). Work even until piece measures 1½" from the beginning, increase 9 sts evenly on last rnd—50 sts. Work even until piece measures 22½" from the beginning.

Shape Bottom

Rnd 1: *Ssk, k6, k2tog; repeat from * to end—40 sts remain.

Rnds 2 and 4: Knit.

Rnd 3: *Ssk, k4, k2tog; repeat from * to end—30 sts remain.

Rnd 5: *Ssk, k2, k2tog; repeat from * to end—20 sts remain.

Rnd 6: *Ssk, k2tog; repeat from * to end—10 sts remain. Break yarn, leaving a long tail. Thread tail through remaining sts, pull tight, and fasten off.

FINISHING

Weave in loose ends.

Felting: Felt Sleeve to desired size (see Special Techniques, page 120). *Note: This yarn tends to felt rather quickly. Keep a close eye on the felting process to ensure your felted work is the correct size to fit the vase you have chosen. The Sleeve will be longer than the vase is tall, until pleating has been completed.*

Place vase upside down on flat surface. Slip wet, felted Sleeve over vase, gently stretching Sleeve to fit. Turn vase right side up. The Sleeve should extend several inches past the top of the vase. Gently push the Sleeve down over the vase to create the pleats. When the top edge of the Sleeve is slightly above the top edge of the vase, pin pleats in place with U or T pins (straight pins will also work). Slightly flare the top of the Sleeve, if desired, by folding the top edge over, creating a small lip at the top. Allow Sleeve to air-dry completely before removing vase.

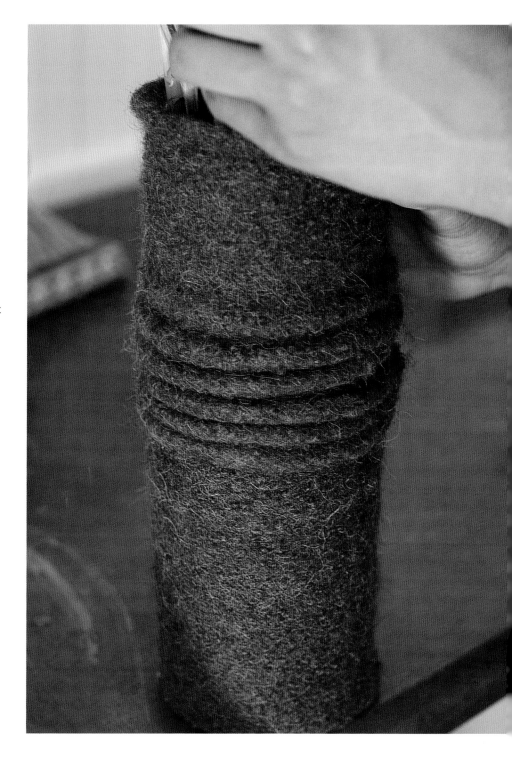

9" circumference × 2¾
(4¼)" high, before felting

Approximately 8½"
circumference × 1¾ (2⅝)"
high, after felting

*Note: Results will depend on
felting conditions and time
spent felting.*

YARN
Louet Riverstone Chunky
Weight (100% wool; 165
yards / 100 grams): 1 hank
#58 Burgundy (Short Vessel)
or #26 Crabapple (Tall
Vessel). *Note: One hank makes
approximately 5 Short and 4
Tall Vessels. If working with
yarn from your stash, you will
need approximately 14 yards
for the Short Vessel and 24
yards for the Tall Vessel.*

NEEDLES
One set of five double-pointed
needles (dpn) size US 10½
(6.5 mm)

Change needle size if
necessary to obtain correct
gauge.

GAUGE
16 sts and 19 rows = 4" (10 cm)
in Stockinette stitch (St st)

Gauge not critical for this
project.

Petite Vessels

*Small containers for small things; the perfect place for rings, earrings, or
loose change, for example.*

VESSELS
CO 30 sts, divide sts among 4 dpns (8-8-7-7). Join for working in
the rnd, being careful not to twist sts; place marker for beginning
of rnd. Begin St st (knit every rnd); work even until piece measures
2¾ (4)" from the beginning.

Shape Bottom
Rnd 1: *Ssk, k2, k2tog; repeat from * to end—20 sts remain.

Rnd 2: Knit

Rnd 3: *Ssk, k2tog; repeat from * to end—10 sts remain. Break
yarn, thread through remaining sts, pull tight, and fasten off.

FINISHING
Weave in loose ends.

Felting: Felt Vessels to desired size (see Special Techniques, page
120). The Vessel can be gently stretched or shaped while it is
wet. You can either do this with your hands or by carefully pulling
the Vessel over a small juice or shot glass. Allow Vessel to air-dry
completely in new shape.

SHOWN TOP TO BOTTOM:
MAT 2, MAT 1

Mikus Linen Placemats

After viewing the serene, monochromatic paintings of artist Eleanore Mikus, I was inspired to try something subtle with my knitting. Here I used linen yarn and a series of rib stitch patterns to capture the interaction of light and shadow.

FINISHED MEASUREMENTS
14" wide × 17" long

YARN
Louet Euroflax Light Worsted Weight (100% wet spun linen; 190 yards / 100 grams): 2 hanks #36 Natural for each Placemat. *Note: Since each Placemat uses only a small amount of the second hank, you only need 3 hanks to work 2 Placemats.*

NEEDLES
One pair straight needles size US 5 (3.75 mm)

Change needle size if necessary to obtain correct gauge.

GAUGE
22 sts and 28 rows = 4" (10 cm) in Stockinette stitch (St st)

MAT 1
CO 83 sts.

Section A
Row 1 (RS): K2, *p7, k1; repeat from * to last st, k1.

Row 2: P2, *k7, p1; repeat from * to last st, p1.

Repeat Rows 1 and 2 until piece measures ½" from the beginning, ending with a WS row.

Section B
Row 1 (RS): K2, *p15, k1; repeat from * to last st, k1.

Row 2: P2, *k15, p1; repeat from * to last st, p1.

Repeat Rows 1 and 2 until piece measures 13" from the beginning, ending with a WS row.

Section C
Row 1 (RS): K2, p1, k2, *(p1, k7); repeat from * to last 6 sts, [p1, k2] twice.

Row 2: P2, k1, p2, *(k1, p7); repeat from * to last 6 sts, [k1, p2] twice.

Repeat Rows 1 and 2 until piece measures 17" from the beginning, ending with a WS row. BO all sts in pattern.

FINISHING
Weave in loose ends. Block pieces to measurements.

MAT 2
CO 76 sts.

Section A
Row 1 (RS): K3, *p6, k2; repeat from * to last st, k1.

Row 2: P3, *k6, p2; repeat from * to last st, p1.

Repeat Rows 1 and 2 until piece measures 2" from the beginning, ending with a WS row.

Section B
Row 1 (RS): K3, *p2, k2; repeat from * to last st, k1.

Row 2: P3, *k2, p2; repeat from * to last st, p1.

Repeat Rows 1 and 2 until piece measures 3½" from the beginning, ending with a WS row.

Section C
Row 1 (RS): P5, *k2, p6; repeat from * to last 7 sts, k2, p5.

Row 2: K5, *p2, k6; repeat from * to last 7 sts, p2, k5.

Repeat Rows 1 and 2 until piece measures 5½" from the beginning, ending with a WS row.

Section D
Row 1 (RS): K3, p5, [k1, p2, k1, p4] 4 times, k1, p4, k27, [p1, k1] twice.

Row 2: [P1, k1] twice, p27, k4, p1, [k4, p1, k2, p1] 4 times, k5, p3.

Repeat Rows 1 and 2 until piece measures 16¼" from the beginning, ending with a WS row.

Section E
Row 1 (RS): K3, p5, [k1, p2, k1, p4] 4 times, k1, p4, [k3, p1, k4, p1] twice, k2, p1, k3, p1, k2, [p1, k1] twice.

Row 2: [P1, k1] twice, p2, k1, p3, k1, p2, [k1, p4, k1, p3] twice, k4, p1, [k4, p1, k2, p1] 4 times, k5, p3.

Repeat Rows 1 and 2 until piece measures 17" from the beginning, ending with a WS row. BO all sts in pattern. Complete as for Mat 1.

FINISHED
MEASUREMENTS
11 1/2" wide × 14" long

YARN
Louet Euroflax Light Worsted
Weight (100% wet spun linen;
190 yards / 100 grams): 2
hanks #35 Mustard

NEEDLES
One pair straight needles size
US 7 (4.5 mm)

One 24" (60 cm) long circular
(circ) needle size US 8 (5 mm)

One 24" (60 cm) long circular
needle size US 7 (4.5 mm)

Change needle size if
necessary to obtain correct
gauge.

NOTIONS
Stitch markers; plastic
sheeting or other waterproof
material large enough to cover
countertop or table; waxed
paper; two 8-ounce bottles
Crafter's Pick Fabric Stiffener
(see Sources for Supplies,
page 124); 5-quart bucket or
bowl; binder clips

Note: If you substitute a
different brand of fabric
stiffener, make sure the brand
you use dries clear. Some
stiffeners leave an uneven
white coating.

GAUGE
16 sts and 32 rows = 4" (10
cm) in Garter st (knit every
row), using larger needle and 2
strands of yarn held together

Serving Tray

I especially enjoy making easy, utilitarian projects with nontraditional materials. For this serving tray, I worked two strands of worsted-weight linen in a combination of Garter and Stockinette stitches, then immersed the floppy fabric in fabric stiffener to make it sturdy enough to be useful.

TRAY

BOTTOM
Using straight needles and 2 strands of yarn held together, CO 46 sts. Begin Garter st; work even until piece measures 14" from the beginning.

SIDES
Using larger circ needle, working around outside edges of Bottom, pick up and knit 1 st for every Garter ridge along left side, place marker (pm), 2 sts in corner, pm, 46 sts along CO edge, pm, 2 sts in corner, pm, 1 st for every Garter ridge along right side, pm, 2 sts in corner, join for working in the rnd, pm for beginning of rnd, work across 46 sts on straight needle, pm, 2 sts in corner, work to beginning of rnd.

Rnds 1 and 3: Change to smaller circ needle. Knit.

Rnd 2: [Knit to marker, slip marker (sm), yo, k2tog, sm] 4 times.

Rnd 4: *K15, BO center 16 sts, [knit to marker, sm, yo, k2tog, sm] twice; repeat from * to end.

Rnd 5: *K15, CO 14 sts over BO sts, [knit to marker, sm, yo, k2tog, sm] twice; repeat from * to end.

Rnd 6: Knit.

Rnd 7: BO all sts knitwise.

FINISHING

Weave in loose ends.

Prepare flat surface, such as counter or tabletop, where you can leave Tray to air-dry undisturbed for several days. Cover surface with plastic or other waterproof material. Cover plastic with layer of waxed paper to keep Tray from sticking to plastic.

Thoroughly mix 12 ounces (1½ cups) fabric stiffener and 4 ounces (½ cup) water in 5-quart bucket or bowl. Immerse Tray in mixture and move around until completely and evenly saturated with stiffener. The knit fabric must absorb an even amount of the stiffening mixture in order to stiffen uniformly.

Lay Tray out flat on wax paper. Using your hands, gently pull Tray into shape. Place binder clips halfway along the long sides and on the bound-off sts under the handle on the short sides to give the sides more structure and prevent them from flopping over.

Remove binder clips when Tray is partially dry. Allow Tray to dry completely. The stiffener will darken the original yarn color slightly. Once the Tray is completely dry, if there are any areas that are not sufficiently stiff or that have dried to a slightly different color, reapply fabric stiffener with a paintbrush where needed or pour directly on the Tray where needed and rub into fabric with your finger.

APPENDIX

Special Techniques

APPLIED I-CORD   Using a double-pointed needle, cast on or pick up required number of sts; working yarn will be at left-hand end of the needle. *Transfer needle with sts to left hand, bring yarn around behind work to right-hand end; using a second double-pointed needle, work sts from right to left as follows, pulling yarn from left to right for the first st: K1, slip 1, k1 from main needle, psso; do not turn. Slide sts to opposite end of needle; repeat from * around entire edge to which I-Cord is to be applied.

BASTING   Work a running stitch using long, loose stitches.

CABLE CO   Make a loop (using a slip knot) with working yarn and place it on left-hand needle (first st CO), knit into slip knot, draw up a loop but do not drop st from left-hand needle; place new loop on left-hand needle; *insert tip of right-hand needle into space between last 2 sts on left-hand needle and draw up a loop; place loop on left-hand needle. Repeat from * for remaining sts to be CO, or for casting on at the end of a row in progress.

FELTING   See page 122.

I-CORD   Using a double-pointed needle, cast on or pick up the required number of sts; the working yarn will be at the left-hand side of the needle. * Transfer needle with sts to left hand, bring yarn around behind work to right-hand side; using a second double-pointed needle, knit sts from right to left, pulling yarn from left to right for first st; do not turn. Slide sts to opposite end of needle; repeat from * until I-Cord is length desired. *Note: After a few rows, tubular shape will become apparent.*

INVISIBLE STITCH   Place two pieces of fabric to be sewn together next to one another. Bring threaded needle out through fold at edge of first piece, and catch a tiny bit of second piece. *Bring needle into fold, move tip of needle over 1/16" or 1/8" within fold, then bring needle out through fold. Catch a tiny bit of the second piece. Pull needle through, and repeat from *.

When working Invisible stitch to sew a zipper into a felted item, work stitches 1/16" or 1/8" from edge of felted fabric and zipper teeth.

JUMP RINGS (OR ANY SPLIT RING)   To open jump ring, hold either side of ring with pliers, with split in ring at top. Gently open ring by pushing left side of ring away from you while pulling right side of ring towards you, creating gap in ring. To close jump ring, gently bring right side of loop back to its original position.

MATTRESS STITCH   Lay two pieces of fabric side by side, with RS's facing up. *Bring threaded needle under

2 strands of yarn near edge of first piece of fabric. Bring needle under 2 corresponding strands of yarn on second piece of fabric. Repeat from *, reinserting needle into a piece of fabric at the point from which the needle last exited the fabric.

READING CHARTS   Unless otherwise specified in the instructions, when working straight, charts are read from right to left for RS rows, from left to right for WS rows. Row numbers are written at the beginning of each row. Numbers on the right indicate RS rows; numbers on the left indicate WS rows. When working circular, all rounds are read from right to left.

RUNNING STITCH   *Insert threaded needle from RS of fabric to WS and back to RS a few times, moving forward each time, then pull through to WS. Repeat from * for desired length of line.

SATIN STITCH   Cover an area with closely spaced straight stitches as follows: Bring threaded needle from WS to RS of fabric at one edge of area to be covered. *At opposite edge of area, bring needle from RS to WS and back to RS, catching smallest possible bit of background fabric. Repeat from *, carefully tensioning the stitches so work lies flat without puckering.

THREE-NEEDLE BO   Place sts to be joined onto two same-size needles; hold pieces to be joined with RSs together and

needles parallel, both pointing to right. Holding both needles in left hand, using working yarn and a third needle the same size or one size larger, insert third needle into first st on front needle, then into first st on back needle; knit these two sts together; * knit next st from each needle together (two sts on right-hand needle); pass first st over second st to BO one st. Repeat from * until one st remains on third needle; cut yarn and fasten off.

FELTING INSTRUCTIONS

1. Choose detergent and set washing machine to following settings: hot water, lowest water level possible, highest agitation level possible.

2. Fill machine's tub with water. Add approximately 1 tablespoon detergent (I use wool washes such as Soak or Eucalan).

3. Place project into machine and begin wash cycle. To speed up felting by increasing friction, include clean jeans, tennis shoes, or tennis balls. Do not use towels; they create lint that will felt into your project.

4. Approximately every 3 to 5 minutes, check on felting progress by removing project from washing machine, gently squeezing out excess moisture, and assessing how close it is to desired size and texture. If necessary, return project to machine, resetting wash cycle. Repeat until project is felted as desired.

   Your project is the most unstable at beginning of felting process. As you check progress (especially at beginning when it is still fairly loose and shapeless), make sure pockets, handles, or other elements are not becoming tangled or sticking to each other. If caught early enough, you can gently pull apart areas that have begun to felt together.

5. Once project is felted to your satisfaction, remove from machine and rinse in sink with lukewarm to cool water. Roll project in a towel to remove excess water. Reshape project if necessary and air-dry on sweater rack. If you don't have a sweater rack, which allows air to circulate on all sides and speeds up the drying process, place project on a folded bath towel to dry.

Note: Do not run felted projects through washer's rinse cycle or place in dryer because these steps can create permanent creases and/or alter the project's finished shape.

Abbreviations

BO   Bind off

Circ   Circular

CO   Cast on

Dpn   Double-pointed needle(s)

K   Knit

K2tog   Knit two sts together.

K3tog   Knit three sts together.

K1-f/b   Knit into front loop and back loop of same st to increase one st.

K1-tbl   Knit one st through the back loop, twisting the st.

M1 (make 1)   With the tip of the left-hand needle inserted from front to back, lift the strand between the two needles onto the left-hand needle; knit the strand through the back loop to increase one st.

P   Purl

P2tog   Purl two sts together.

P1-f/b   Purl into front loop and back loop of same st to increase one st.

Pm   Place marker

Psso (pass slipped stitch over)   Pass slipped st on right-hand needle over the sts indicated in the instructions, as in binding off.

Rnd   Round

RS   Right side

Sm   Slip marker

Ssk (slip, slip, knit)   Slip the next two sts to the right-hand needle one at a time as if to knit; return them back to left-hand needle one at a time in their new orientation; knit them together through the back loop(s).

St(s)   Stitch(es)

Tbl   Through the back loop

Tog   Together

WS   Wrong side

Yo (yarnover)   Bring yarn forward (to purl position), then place it in position to work next st. If next st is to be knit, bring yarn over needle and knit; if next st is to be purled, bring yarn over needle and then forward again to purl position and purl. Work yarnover in pattern on next row unless instructed otherwise.

Sources for Supplies

YARN

Alchemy Yarns of Transformation
P.O. Box 1080
Sebastopol, CA 95473
707-823-3276
alchemyyarns.com

Berroco
14 Elmdale Road
P.O. Box 367
Uxbridge, MA 01569
508-278-2527
berroco.com

Blue Sky Alpacas
P.O. Box 88
Cedar, MN 55011
888-460-8862
blueskyalpacas.com

Brown Sheep Company
100662 County Road 16
Mitchell, NE 69357
800-826-9136
brownsheep.com

Cascade Yarns
1224 Andover Park East
Tukwila, WA 98188
cascadeyarns.com

Classic Elite
122 Western Avenue
Lowell, MA 01851
800-343-0308
classiceliteyarns.com

**Fairmount Fibers
(Manos del Uruguay)**
915 N. 28th Street
Philadelphia, PA 19130
888-566-9970
fairmountfibers.com

**Knitting Fever (ONLine Yarns
and Ella Rae Classic)**
P.O. Box 336
315 Bayview Avenue
Amityville, NY 11701
516-546-3600
knittingfever.com

Lanaknits Designs
320 Vernon Street, Suite 3B
Nelson, British Columbia
V1L4E4, Canada
888-301-0011
hempforknitting.com

**Leigh Radford / Lantern Moon
(Silk Gelato)**
800-530-4170
lanternmoon.com
leighradford.com

Louet North America
P.O. Box 267
Ogdensburg, NY 13669
613-925-4502
louet.com

Malabrigo Yarn
Haiti 1500
Montevideo 12800
Uruguay
786-866-6187 (U.S.)
malabrigoyarn.com

Misti International, Inc.
P.O. Box 2532
Glen Ellyn, IL 60138
888-776-9276
mistialpaca.com

Muench Yarns & Buttons
1323 Scott Street
Petaluma, CA 94954
800-773-9276
muenchyarns.com

ShibuiKnits
1101 SW Alder Street
Portland, OR 97205
503-227-0009
shibuiknits.com

Westminster Fibers
(Nashua Handknits
and Rowan Yarns)
165 Ledge Street
Nashua, NH 03060
800-445-9276
westminsterfibers.com

OTHER SUPPLIES
The Adhesive Products, Inc.
(Api's Crafter's Pick
Fabric Stiffener)
520 Cleveland Avenue
Albany, CA 94710
510-526-7616
crafterspick.com

Dava Bead and Trade
(beads and jewelry-making
supplies)
2121 NE Broadway
Portland, OR 97232
503-288-3991
davabeadandtrade.com

Fashion Hot
(hot water bottles)
480-459-8831
fashionhot.com

Ghees.com
(bag handles and frames)

Jewelry.com
(sterling silver jump rings)

Michaels Stores
(Jewelry Essentials findings)
michaels.com

Oregon Leather Company
(leather supplies)
110 NW Second Avenue
Portland, OR 97209
800-634-8033
oregonleatherco.com

Clothing on
pages 23 and 72:
Seaplane
827 NW 23rd
Portland, OR 97210
503-234-2409
e-seaplane.com

Fence on pages 26 and 68
designed by Brian Thompsen
(b_kindness@hotmail.com).

INSPIRATION
Eleanore Mikus
eleanoremikus.com

Josef Albers
albersfoundation.org

Acknowledgments

I am very grateful to the gifted group of people who have contributed their time and talents to this book: Melanie Falick, my editor, whose confidence in me inspires me to do my best work; John Mulligan, whose beautiful photography fills the pages of this third book we've worked on together; and Kevin Wells, photography assistant, whose good humor and good taste in music kept the photo shoot fun and productive.

Thanks to models Nash Armisted, Carma Ferrier, Karen Lounsbury, Sadie Mulligan, Kacy Owens, Britta Pool, Brian Thompsen, and Kate Towers; to Claudine Ebel for expert hair and makeup and to Karen Ford and John Dingler for graciously allowing us into their garden for photography.

Thanks to editor Liana Allday for her hard work and dedication, to Sue McCain for her expert technical editing and good humor, and to graphic designer Anna Christian, whose creativity and attention to detail have added so much to this book.

Special thanks to OCAC instructors Michelle Ross, Georgiana Nehl, and Heidi Schwegler for introducing me to new sources of inspiration.

I must also thank the following companies who so generously provided yarn for the projects: Alchemy Yarns of Transformation, Berroco, Blue Sky Alpacas, Brown Sheep Company, Cascade Yarns, Classic Elite, Fairmount Fibers (Manos del Uruguay), Knitting Fever, Lanaknits, Lantern Moon, Louet North America, Malabrigo Yarn, Misti International, Muench Yarns, ShibuiKnits, and Westminster Fibers (Nashua Handknits and Rowan Yarns).

Special thanks to family and friends—your ongoing support and encouragement make it possible for me to stay on my creative path.